Rethinking Public Services

Rajiv Prabhakar

First published in 2006 by
PALGRAVE MACMILLAN
Houndmills, Basingstoke, Hampshire RG21 6XS and
175 Fifth Avenue, New York, N.Y. 10010
Companies and representatives throughout the world

PALGRAVE MACMILLAN is the global academic imprint of the Palgrave Macmillan division of St. Martin's Press, LLC and of Palgrave Macmillan Ltd. Macmillan® is a registered trademark in the United States, United Kingdom and other countries. Palgrave is a registered trademark in the European Union and other countries.

ISBN-13: 978–1–4039–2156–7 hardback
ISBN-10: 1–4039–2156–3 hardback
ISBN-13: 978–1–4039–2157–4 paperback
ISBN-10: 1–4039–2157–1 paperback

This book is printed on paper suitable for recycling and made from fully managed and sustained forest sources.

A catalogue record for this book is available from the British Library.

A catalog record for this book is available from the Library of Congress.

Printed and bound in China

GOVERNMENT BEYOND THE CENTRE

SERIES EDITORS: GERRY STOKER AND DAVID WILSON

Published

Richard Batley and Gerry Stoker (eds)
Local Government in Europe

Bas Denters and Lawrence E. Rose (eds)
Comparing Local Governance

Sue Goss
Making Local Governance Work

Clive Gray
Government Beyond the Centre

John Gyford
Citizens, Consumers and Councils

Richard kerley
Managing in Local Government

Desmond king and Gerry Stoker (eds)
Rethinking Local Democracy

Steve Leach, John Stewart and Kieron Walsh
The Changing Organisation and Management of Local Governance

Arthur Midwinter
Local Government in Scotland

Christopher Pollift, Johnston Birchall and Keith Putman
Decentralising Public Service Management

Rajiv Prabhakar
Rethinking Public Services

Lawrence Pratchett
Local Democracy in Britain

Lawrence Pratchett and David Wilson (eds)
Local Democracy and Local Government

John Stewart
The Nature of British Local Government

Gerry Stoker
Transforming Local Governance

Gerry Stoker (ed.)
The New Management of British Local Governance

Gerry Stoker (ed.)
The New Politics of British Local Governance

Gerry Stoker and David Wilson (eds)
British Local Government in the 2000s

Helen Sullivan and Chris Skelcher
Working Across Boundaries

Tony Travers
The Politics of London

David Wilson and Chris Game
Local Government in the United Kingdom (4th edn)

Perri 6, Diana Leat, Kimberly Seltzer and Gerry Stoker
Towards Holistic Governance

Rajiv Prabhakar
The Future of Public Services

Forthcoming

Steve Martin
The Transformation of Public Services

Books by the same author

Stakeholding and New Labour (2003) Palgrave Macmillan

GOVERNMENT BEYOND THE CENTRE

SERIES EDITORS: GERRY STOKER AND DAVID WILSON

The world of sub-central governance and administration – including local authorities, quasi-governmental bodies and the agencies of public–private partnerships – has seen massive changes in the United Kingdom and other western democracies. The original aim of the **Government Beyond the Centre** series was to bring the study of this often-neglected world into the mainstream of social science research, applying the spotlight of critical analysis to what had traditionally been the preserve of institutional public administration approaches.

The replacement of traditional models of government by new models of governance has affected central government, too, with the contracting out of many traditional functions, the increasing importance of relationships with devolved and supranational authorities, and the emergence of new holistic models based on partnership and collaboration.

This series focuses on the agenda of change in governance both at sub-central level and in the new patterns of relationships surrounding the core executive. Its objective is to provide up-to-date and informative accounts of the new forms of management and administration and the structures of power and influence that are emerging, and of the economic, political and ideological forces that underlie them.

The series will be of interest to students and practitioners in central and local government, public management and social policy, and all those interested in the reshaping of the governmental institutions which have a daily and major impact on our lives.

Government Beyond the Centre
Series Standing Order
ISBN 0–333–71696–5 hardback
ISBN 0–333–69337–X paperback
(*outside North America only*)

You can receive future titles in this series as they are published by placing a standing order. Please contact your bookseller or, in the case of difficulty, write to us at the address below with your name and address, the title of the series and the ISBN quoted above.

Customer Services Department, Macmillan Distribution Ltd,
Houndmills, Basingstoke, Hampshire RG21 6XS, England

To Helen, Maya and Arun

Contents

Acknowledgements

I have acquired a variety of debts during the writing of this book. This book was written while I held a Ludwig Lachmann fellowship at the Department of Philosophy, Logic and Scientific Method at the London School of Economics. I am very grateful for financial support from Charlottenburg Trust which funded this fellowship. The Department of Philosophy was a very supportive environment in which to work. I would particularly like to thank the departmental convenor Colin Howson for all his help and support throughout the fellowship.

I am very grateful for comments received on successive drafts of this work from Gerry Stoker as series editor and my publisher Steven Kennedy as well as comments from an anonymous reviewer. Although I have not followed all their advice, their comments have certainly helped to shape and improve the book. Of course, all remaining errors are my own. I have also benefited from seminar presentations at the London School of Economics, the Institute of Political and Economic Governance at the University of Manchester and the University of Strathclyde. A series of seminars run by the think-tank Catalyst on the reform of public services proved a valuable forum to think about some of the themes of this book. I would like to thank Martin McIvor and Catherine Needham at Catalyst for inviting me to participate in these sessions. I also learned much from discussions held at the New Local Government Network and Mutuo.

I would like to thank the editors of the following journals for permission to draw (often in heavily revised form) on some of the material I have had previously published: 'New Localism and Public Sector Workers', *Renewal*, 13(1) (2005); 'Do Public Interest Companies form a Third Way in Public Services?', *British Journal of Politics and International Relations*, 6(3), 353–369 (2004); 'Commercialisation or Citizenship?', *Politics*, 24(3), 215–220 (2004); 'Does the new localism threaten equality?', *Renewal*, 11(4), 73–80 (2003) and 'Capability, responsibility and human capital', *Political Quarterly*, 73(1), 51–57, 2002.

Finally, I am very grateful to my family and friends. Special thanks go to my wife and children. I would also like to thank my mother, father, brother, Ben Cowell, Preethike Dias, Cormac Hollingsworth and David Richardson. I am grateful to them all for providing diversionary activities.

1 Introduction

In this book I aim to rethink the way in which public services are organised and run. My main aim is to suggest a response that breaks with 'states versus markets' debates that have shaped thinking for much of the twentieth century (Hirst 1996; Bowles and Gintis 1998; Ackerman and Alstott 1999; Brown 2003; Gamble and Wright 2004). The 'state-centred approach' suggests that the ideal is for the state to both fund and deliver public services. The 'free market model' insists that mainly private companies competing with each other in the marketplace should ideally do the funding and delivery of public services. Put simply, my argument is that there is now a case for trying to escape these alternatives and explore the ways in which state, civil society and market might usefully combine in the organisation of public services. This is driven by the need to respond to issues of state failure and market failure, as well as be sensitive to the changes wrought by globalisation. I do not think that state, civil society and market can combine easily in some happy family dance. For example, tensions exist between central and local bodies over the proper scope for local autonomy. I am also aware that trying to introduce new solutions can also usher in new problems. However, I believe that the limitations associated with the existing approaches to public services provide grounds for examining alternative options.

My exploration leads me into the territory of the 'third way'. The third way emerged during the 1990s as various commentators sought to grapple with the challenges posed by globalisation and the New Right. The third way denotes an approach that breaks from a state-centred and free market public policy. The 'third way' has provoked international interest among politicians and policy-makers alike. In the United States, it has attracted support from individuals such as the former President Bill Clinton and the academic and former US Secretary of State of Labor Robert Reich (1999) as well as bodies such as the Democratic Leadership Council and the think-tank, the Progressive Policy Institute. In a speech given to a conference held in London in 2003 on progressive governance, Bill Clinton stated that the, 'Third way should be the dominant mode of thinking about change in the 21st century' (Clinton 2003). Clinton and the Democratic Leadership Council hosted a roundtable discussion in Washington on 25 April 1999 on the third way. This was attended by British Prime Minister Tony Blair, German Chancellor Gerhard Schroeder, Dutch Prime Minister Wim Kok and Italian Prime Minister Massimo D'Alema. Outside the United States, intellectuals such as Anthony Giddens (1998, 2000) and politicians such as Blair and Schroeder (Blair 1998; Blair and Schroeder 1999) have played a role in propagating third way ideas.

The third way provokes much critical commentary (Economist 1998; Hall 1998; Faux 1999; Giddens 2000; Callinicos 2003). Perhaps the most common criticism is that the third way is vague and lacks substance. For example, Jeff Faux (1999) argues that it is difficult to detect a definite meaning to the third way. Instead, it is an amorphous political project that stretches to cover a very wide range of different programmes. Stuart Hall (1998) adds that once one goes beyond the vagueness of third way and studies the actual policies pursued by politicians who espouse the third way, one finds in fact an accommodation with free market assumptions and policies.

Although I have various reservations about the term third way, it is nonetheless the case that the arguments presented in this book suggest that this concept is not devoid of content. One of my concerns with the third way is that this term maps out a large space that is compatible with a range of distinct, and possibly contradictory, projects. Consequently, it seems more accurate to talk of third *ways* rather than *the* third way. I also do not think the third way marks a kind of 'year zero'. Throughout the twentieth century, there have been figures who have sought to explore the space beyond the state and free markets. Examples include R.H. Tawney's advocacy of ethical socialism as an antidote to the rise of the acquisitive society (Tawney 1948) and Paul Hirst's support for associative democracy. The third way marks the latest twist of a particular historical tradition rather than something completely novel. In spite of these (and other) reservations, I shall persist in this book to use the term third way. I do this because this term serves as a convenient and well-known shorthand for the terrain I am exploring.

The argument in this book overlaps with two of the emerging strands within the contemporary third way. Stuart White (1998) argues that several currents can be identified within third way space. One strain gives attention to developing mutual forms of organisation. This looks at how the governance of organisations can be altered to incorporate a greater role for those who are materially affected by the performance of the organisation (Fung and Wright 2001; Mayo and Moore 2001; Wainwright 2003). A different thread explores how the role of the state can be changed from the role of direct provider to a stance where it acts as an enabler or guarantor of services. Anthony Giddens (1998, 2000) is a contributor to this line of thought. This can be seen in his arguments for a 'social investment' state. The version of public services put forward in this book adds to both of these currents. A larger role envisaged for local bodies in the delivery of public services resonates with the attempt to fashion new models of the state. Also, the role that stakeholding plays within such local institutions means that this also intersects with the interest shown in mutuality.

Current debates

Public services face a series of challenges today. These issues provide much of the impetus behind the current attention among academics, politicians and policy-makers about how public services are organised and run. While the below is not a list of all the issues that public services face, they nevertheless sketch out some of the more important challenges.

User expectations

Public services have to cope with an increase in the expectations of those who use these services. This means that people are more demanding of the services that they receive, expecting a higher quality of service and services more tailored to their needs (Coulter 2002; Blendon and DesRoches 2003; Blank and Burau 2004). Although there is room for debate about the extent to which expectations are rising, there is evidence that points to the dissatisfaction that significant proportions feel with the current state of public services. For example, a series of surveys conducted by the School of Public Health at Harvard University in conjunction with the Commonwealth Fund of New York and Harris Interactive Incorporated provide an indication of the concerns of users of health within the United States, Canada, Australia, New Zealand and the United Kingdom (Donelan et al. 1999; Donelan et al. 2000; Blendon et al. 2002; Blendon et al. 2003).[1] Robert Blendon, Cathy Schoen, Catherine DesRoches, Robin Osborn and Kinga Zapert (2003) highlight some of the concerns of the chronically sick or those with acute care needs. These authors argue that the experience of the chronically sick provide a bellwether of how care systems are working. The chronically sick are heavily involved with the different parts of the health system – such as contact with physicians, prescription drugs and waiting times – and as such their views can provide a useful snapshot of how health services are functioning. As part of the project, these researchers studied the views of

roughly 1000 individuals in each country. These included people who had
had a serious injury or required major surgery in the past two years. These
authors found that sizeable minorities within each country had a negative
view of the overall performance of the health system. Those who were
either not very or not at all satisfied went from 31 per cent in the United
Kingdom, 35 per cent in Australia, 36 per cent in Canada, 44 per cent in the
United States and 48 per cent in New Zealand. Worries about the cost of
treatment and inadequate coverage of healthcare were the top concerns of
those in the United States, shortage of health professionals or beds was
expressed as the main problem in Canada, Australians cited waiting lists
and hospital shortages as the principal deficiencies, and those in Britain and
New Zealand complained most about waiting times. Karen Donelan, Robert
Blendon, Cathy Schoen, Karen Davis and Katherine Binns (1999) report on
dissatisfaction within the general population within these five countries. In
1998, they organised interviews with a representative sample of around 750
individuals within each country. The researchers found that only a minority
think that the health system is working well and require minor changes to
make it work better. Those advocating little or no change range from 25 per
cent of the sample in the United Kingdom, 20 per cent in Canada, 19 per cent
in Australia, 17 per cent in the United States and 9 per cent in New Zealand.
The remainder of the sample believe that the system needs fundamental
changes or complete rebuilding. Concerns focus on issues such as lack of
adequate funding (United Kingdom), access to care (United States) and
waiting times (Australia).

Similar sentiments are found elsewhere. The Stockholm network (a
service organisation for Europe's market-oriented think-tanks) commis-
sioned the polling body Populus to conduct a European-wide survey of attitudes to healthcare. A total of 8000 people were questioned in the following
eight countries: Britain, the Czech Republic, France, Germany, Italy, the
Netherlands, Sweden and Spain. Individuals numbering 1000 were
interviewed over the telephone in each of these countries between 26 January
and 22 February 2004. Each country's sample consisted of people over
15 years of age who were representative of the age, gender and regional composition of the nation. Participants were asked to comment on the state of the
national health services and how they feel these services compare with the
systems in other countries. In an overview to the study, Helen Disney (2004)
argues that despite important national differences, it is possible to place
these different countries in one of two broad categories. The first consists of
tax-funded government monopolies or 'Beveridgean' systems. Here, the state is
the dominant funder and provider of health. Disney argues that Britain, the

Czech Republic, Sweden, Spain and Italy belong in this camp. The second comprises social insurance or 'Bismarckian' systems that put more weight on public and private funding and a mixed system of provision. Disney places France, Germany and the Netherlands in this category. The results of the survey provoke concern for both of these types. One set of questions looked at how important people rate having a short time between diagnosis and treatment, being treated at a time and place of their choosing, being treated with the latest medicine and technology, having sufficient information to make informed choices, and being treated by a doctor of their choice. The survey measured the difference between values and reality. A 'delivery deficit' is defined as the percentage of respondents who ranked the item in question as important minus the percentage of respondents who felt the health service is delivering a good level of service (the greater the deficit, the wider the gap between values and experience). All the countries surveyed recorded a substantial value for the delivery deficit. Britain performs worst on this dimension, having an average value of 63 over the five issues mentioned above. Germany performs best, with an average delivery deficit of 37. This is followed by France on 39. When citizens were asked to compare their health systems with those in other countries, French respondents suffered the least and members of the Czech Republic suffered the most on what is dubbed an index of inferiority.

Rising costs

Public services have to accommodate rising costs. For example, in the United States the Congressional Budget Office predicts that combined spending on social security and health (covering the medicare and medicaid programmes) is due to more than double from its present level of 8 per cent of gross domestic product to reach 20 per cent by 2075 (Krugman 2005). These costs are driven by two important factors. The first is demographic change (Pierson 2001; Blank and Burau 2004; Kotlikoff and Burns 2004). The basic idea here is that a shrinking population of younger people will have to bear the rising costs of providing for a growing elderly population. The World Bank (1994) notes that while around half a billion of the world's population was aged 60 or over in 1990 (9 per cent of the world's population), it is estimated that in 2030 this number will rise to around 1.4 billion people (16 per cent). The Organization for Economic Co-operation and Development (1996) states that the number of people aged 75 or over is set to double between 1990 and 2030. At the same time, there has been a fall in birth rates, which means fewer people of working age (between 15 and 64 years old) are entering the labour force. The 'dependency ratio' – the ratio of the non-working to the working population – is projected to rise from 19 per cent in 1990 to 37 per cent in 2030 (Organization for Economic Co-operation and Development 1996). Laurence Kotlikoff and Scott Burns (2004) say that in the United States the dependency ratio of the over 65s to those between 20 and 64 is set to rise from 21.1 per cent to 35.5 per cent between 2000 and 2030. Whereas there will be 35.5 million people in the United States aged 65 or over in 2000, by 2030 this is set to increase to 69.4 million. This growth creates an upwards pressure on costs. Various services will have to be expanded – such as increased medical services, long-term residential care and pension provision – and this expansion will raise costs. In a system in which the taxes of those in work are used to help provide for public services, the increase in costs will put upwards pressure on taxes. A fall in the working age population will intensify this pressure on taxes: fewer younger people will have to pay more. Laurence Kotlikoff and Scott Burns say that in the United States this could mean that corporate and personal taxes could double. They say that demographic change is one of the most pressing problems facing public services, and they characterise this as a coming generational storm.

Second, technological change is putting pressure on costs (Blendon and DesRoches 2003; Blank and Burau 2004; Krugman 2005). Developments in information technology and computing is expanding the range of things that public services can do. Technological innovation is usually not cheap, and so this feeds into higher costs. For example, implanted cardiac devices have been shown to be highly effective in treating people with heart trouble. The costs of such devices, however, are expensive (Krugman 2005). Paul Krugman (2005) argues that technological change, particularly in relation to medicine, creates more of a problem than demographic change. He writes that the 'main reason health care is continuing to absorb a larger share of the economy is innovation: that the range of things that medicine can do keeps increasing' (Krugman 2005, 10). He says that although steps may be taken to contain costs, the success of this strategy is not guaranteed. He states that, 'In the long run, in fact, it may be impossible to resolve' (Krugman 2005, 11).

New Right critique

Public services have faced a serious intellectual assault over much of the recent past. Traditionally, the idea of 'market failure' has provided a basic

rationale for the existence of public services (Grout and Stevens 2003).
'Public goods' are a standard example of an instance in which such a failure
occurs. These goods are characterised by two key qualities. First, they are
'non-rivalrous'. This means that any one individual's consumption of
the good does not diminish the amount available for others. Second, it is difficult to exclude those who have not paid for the good from consuming the
commodity. Typical examples of public goods include national defence and
street lighting. Market failure occurs because profit-seeking companies may
not be motivated to provide such goods because they anticipate that they
will encounter a large number of people who will consume but avoid paying
for the commodity. Corporations may assume that they face little prospect
of recouping the costs of providing the goods because of such 'free-rider'
problems. Although market failure has often referred to situations where a
system of private funding and control does not deliver an efficient service,
it can also be construed more broadly to include equity or distributional
goals. Amartya Sen (1987) points out that achieving an efficient allocation
of resources does not guarantee that resources will be distributed equally.
Within orthodox economics, efficiency in a system of distribution and
allocation is achieved when it is not possible to allocate resources in such a
way that the welfare of any particular individual can be improved without
making someone else worse off. Efficiency can arise in a variety of ways. It
is possible that efficiency can occur when one person within society has
access to the total resources of a community while all other members of the
population have nothing. If the person who receives all the resources of a
community is not satiated by this experience, then this state of affairs is efficient because any redistribution away from the sole owner will reduce his or
her welfare (thus it is not possible to make someone better off without making someone else worse off). Sen notes, however, that it is possible to construct alternative patterns of distribution that yield an efficient allocation of
resources. One might want to extend the notion of market failure so that it
takes account of how resources are distributed, as well as whether or not
efficiency is achieved.

During the latter part of the twentieth century, this notion of market
failure has been countered by the idea of 'government failure'. The most
important of these critics are associated with the 'New Right'. The New
Right is a term that has to be handled with some care. This label is used to
group together people who have important differences in the sort of political programmes they endorse. Four main strands of New Right thought can
be identified (Harris 1998). First, the 'public choice' wing, which
encompasses figures such as James Buchanan and Gordon Tullock (1962),

contends that the welfare state is built on flawed assumptions about human motivations. Buchanan and Tullock argue that the welfare state is grounded on the idea that people are virtuous: public servants are motivated by an ethic of service while users are driven by responsibility. Public choice thinkers argue that this neglects the role that self-interest plays in all human motivation. This matters because faulty assumptions about human motivations give rise to badly designed public services. Second, 'Austrian school' thinkers such as Friedrich Hayek contend that social democrats do not appreciate the radical difficulties that the state faces in gaining access to the knowledge that is needed to develop appropriate policy responses. Third, libertarians such as Robert Nozick (1974) argue that the compulsory redistribution that is inherent in the welfare state is a fundamental attack on a person's freedom, as it undermines the legitimate ownership claims each one has have over the fruits of his or her own labour. Fourth, neoconservatives thinkers such as Lawrence Mead (1986) suggest that rather than resolving welfare problems, state intervention has only succeeded in guaranteeing that the problems are prolonged because the state cultivates a dependency culture whereby individuals rely on the state to alleviate their problems rather than take the steps they alone can take to overcome their problems. Clearly, the New Right groups together a disparate range of arguments that have different implications. Sometimes these strands oppose each other. For example, free market reforms can undermine the social ties that are important for neoconservatives (Marquand 1988). What unites all the members of the New Right, however, is a commitment and endorsement of the free market (Faulks 1998; Harris 1998; Marquand 1988). Keith Faulks comments that all

the thinkers of the New Right oppose the social liberal consensus established in the post-war period, all are highly wary of socialism and welfare statism, all support the market as the best creator of wealth and guarantee of personal freedom (Faulks 1998, 53).

New Right arguments were sidelined in the decades immediately after the end of the Second World War. However, they gathered weight during the 1970s with the difficulties governments encountered in controlling unemployment and inflation (Skidelsky 1996; King and Wood 1999). The collapse of central planning in the former Soviet Union and Eastern Europe during the late 1980s and early 1990s provided further ammunition for the New Right. At the level of ideas, New Right thinking began to set the terms of political trade. David Marquand comments that the, 'New Right paradigm shaped the political agenda and controlled the intellectual weather' (Marquand 1996, 8). Many progressives began to accept the gravity of the challenges that the New Right directed at the state. One sign of this dominance can be seen in the complaints made by parts of the left that rather than contesting New Right principles, many reformists have played a politics of 'catch-up' whereby they have increasingly absorbed New Right assumptions into their political programmes (Hay 1999). New Right ideas have also had an impact on policy. Gerald Holtham and John Kay state that the

> most important change in thinking about economic policy of the last 20 years has been the revival of belief in market forces. It has resulted in sweeping changes to many of the former and current economic institutions of the state. In the OECD countries, the changes have gone furthest and been most systematic in the United Kingdom and in New Zealand, but many other countries have joined in (Holtham and Kay 1994, 1).

Caution has to be exercised when linking ideas and public policy. Policy is shaped by a variety of factors, only one of which is ideology. Electoral calculations, unexpected events, a clash of personalities all play a role in moulding policy. In addition, any one set of ideas has to compete with other sets in the wider market for ideas. Also, politicians sometimes reach for an idea after they have already embarked on a policy in order to provide some belated justification for the approach they are adopting. All of this introduces caveats in any attempt to 'read off' policy towards public services from New Right prescriptions. Although Holtham and Kay arguably exaggerate when they refer to sweeping changes in policy across the globe, it does seem plausible to suggest that New Right ideas have an important impact on the organisation of public services in many countries. Holtham and Kay point to the withdrawal of the state from production. State-owned enterprises in countries such as France, Japan, Italy and Sweden have been sold off through privatisation programmes. They also note that market ideas have been injected into the welfare state. Executive agencies were hived off from central government, for example, and are forced to compete with one another.

Globalisation

Globalisation is the subject of a very large, and ever growing, literature (Giddens 1998; Held et al. 1999; Scholte 2000). Globalisation is a complex concept, composed of a number of different elements. The economic aspects of globalisation have probably attracted the most attention in recent times. Accounts of economic globalisation usually highlight the importance of three main changes within the global economy. First, attention is drawn to a rapid increase in the volume and speed of financial transactions conducted across the globe. Facilitated by developments in information and communications technology, global capital is more mobile than at any time in the past. Second, global trade has intensified with the creation of new trade links between different nations as well as through a deepening of the ties that already exist. Third, multinationals play an increasingly important role in the nature of the production process. These companies have workforces that span different countries (Held et al. 1999; Scholte 2000; Pierson 2001). Although economic aspects of this phenomenon are important, globalisation is not only about economics. Globalisation has important social dimensions, and this concerns the impetus it provides to a more plural and complex society (Giddens 1998; Jayasuriya 2000; Scholte 2000). Some commentators allege that this social side to globalisation is the most significant aspect of this phenomenon. Anthony Giddens writes that globalisation, 'is not only, or even primarily about economic interdependence, but about the transformation of time and space in our lives' (Giddens 1998, 30–31). Developments in computer and information technologies have increased the information that can be made readily available to people, and individuals can communicate more easily with people in different parts of the world through the Internet and e-mail. Individuals can more easily adopt divergent lifestyles, contributing to a more plural and complex society.

Of course, care must be exercised not to exaggerate the importance of the above changes. The proposition that globalisation is unprecedented or completely changing economic and social structures does not seem to be tenable (Hirst and Thompson 1996; Pierson 2001; Hay 2004). Paul Hirst and Grahame Thompson (1996) argue that on any of the main dimensions that are used to analyse economic globalisation, it can be shown that there was at least as much activity on these fronts at previous points in history. They claim, for example, that the system of international trade before 1914 was more extensive than that witnessed today. They argue in fact that global economic ties tended to dissipate after the end of the First World War and that the current increases in global economic activity represents a return to the pre-1914 global economy (Hirst and Thompson 1996). In addition, the consequences of globalisation can be exaggerated. Some commentators believe that globalisation spells the demise of state intervention (Ohmae 1990). For example, if a country is to stimulate investment within the domestic economy, then it must offer firms an attractive environment in which to operate. Corporations seek to contain their costs and so will invest in those countries which offer low tax rates and offer less in the way of regulation of business (such as the rules governing the treatment of workers or the environmental impact of corporate activities). Downward pressure is placed on state spending. At its worst, countries will have to offer a residual welfare system (Pierson 2001). It is difficult to square doubts, however, over the viability of state expenditure on public services with the substantial sums that the state still spends across a wide variety of countries today. Colin Hay (2004) surveys state expenditure as a proportion of gross domestic product for the period from 1960 to 2000 for the following countries: Australia, Austria, Belgium, Canada, Denmark, Finland, France, Germany, Ireland, Italy, Japan, the Netherlands, Norway, New Zealand, Sweden, Switzerland, the United Kingdom and the United States. In this period, the trend of state spending as a percentage of gross domestic product has been broadly upwards. In 1960, state expenditure as a proportion of gross domestic product fell within a range of around 18–35 per cent (Switzerland and Belgium exhibited the lowest and highest proportions, respectively). In 2000, the range went from around 30–50 per cent (Japan and Sweden had the lowest and highest proportions, respectively).

While the above reflections provide a useful corrective to a view that globalisation is unprecedented or is tearing up existing economic or social structures, the challenges that globalisation is posing to the organisation of public services should not be overlooked (Giddens 1998; Scholte 2000; Pierson 2001). On the one hand, globalisation creates a set of issues that cut across national boundaries. One component of this relates to the increased ease with which people and goods can, and do, travel across the globe. Within health, this increases the potential spread of communicable diseases or illnesses. The spread of 'transborder health risks' such as HIV/AIDS and the SARS virus point to the emergence of global health issues. Although the spread of diseases such as the bubonic plague in Europe during the Middle Ages illustrate that the spread of communicable diseases across national boundaries today are nothing new, the likely spread of such diseases has been intensified by the increased levels of global travel (Collin and Lee 2003). Within crime, globalisation has made it easier for criminal networks to conduct illegal activities – such as trading in drugs or laundering money – across different countries. These global problems demand some form of global intervention. On the other hand, globalisation makes the task of governing society within national boundaries more complex and difficult. For example, globalisation provides a boost to consumer society.

Consumerism involves people choosing goods or services in the market-place and offering cash in exchange for these items. Although consumerism existed before globalisation, it has been enhanced by globalisation. Jan Aarte Scholte notes that, 'Globalization has made consumerism a far stronger force for the twenty-first century than it would otherwise have been' (Scholte 2000, 115). Technological developments have made the process of buying goods much easier than in the past. People can use the Internet to purchase goods from different countries, thus adding to the product mix available in domestic markets. Globalisation has also led to the creation of global brands that stimulate demand in different countries. Technology also makes it easier to develop a wider range of products, enabling goods or services to be increasingly tailored to individual preferences. This spurt to consumer society links in with public expectations of public services (Ham and Alberti 2002; Corry et al. 2003). Chris Ham and George Alberti (2002) argue that people compare the standard of service and variety experienced in the private realm with that provided in the public realm and expect public services to deliver comparable levels of service. This means heightened public expectations of public services.

These debates about public services feed into broader debates within politics and economics. The concern about the link between economic glob-alisation and the retrenchment of the welfare state is part of a broader dis-cussion about the impact of globalisation on modern life. Similarly, the attention to user dissatisfaction taps into a wider debate about civic partici-pation (Fung and Wright 2001; Mayo and Moore 2001; Crouch 2003). Links can also be drawn between the above debates. A connection between economic globalisation and user dissatisfaction has already been noted. Similarly, globalisation is often used to bolster New Right arguments. The view here is that global economic changes mandate the acceptance of free market assumptions (Hirst 1999b; Leys 2001). Although the above is not an exhaustive list of all the factors stimulating the present interest in public services, and the different debates are not mutually exclusive, they highlight some of the salient issues facing public services today.

The centralised state

The above indicates that public services today face a series of important challenges. These challenges provide a case for re-examining the assump-tions used to shape how public services are funded and delivered. Of course, exploring the theoretical assumptions that inform public services is not the only thing of importance when examining public services. Public services are also shaped by the interactions between competing interests as well as the legacy from the previous arrangements for public services. While the significance of these other issues ought to be recognised, the task of rethinking public services is an important one. Investigating these assumptions can help bring coherence to different areas of policy, setting out, for example, how policy initiatives might develop in a consistent fashion. Rethinking can also help set out the basic options or choices on offer.

During the twentieth century, public services have often been associated with the centralised state. Paul Hirst says that, 'For the better part of a century, the growing and changing bundle of public services denoted by the term "welfare" has been identified with state provision by supporters and critics alike' (Hirst 1996, 158). Similarly, Julian Le Grand comments that in,

> most countries, the state has historically played a major role in both the finance and delivery of social services such as education, health care, housing, and social care. Often this role has taken the form of some kind of state bureaucracy actually providing the service, while simultaneously using state revenues to subsidise it such that it is free (or offered at highly subsidised prices) at the point of use (Le Grand 2003b, 3).

The role of the state is captured in works such as T.H. Marshall's *Citizenship and Social Class*. This work provides an influential account of the evolution of citizenship since the seventeenth century. According to Marshall, the concept of citizenship changed over time so that it came to embrace not just civil and political rights (such as freedom of expression and the right to vote) but also rights to social resources such as health and education. Marshall argues that citizenship altered to cover these social rights during the twentieth century. Marshall continues that the key principle underpinning these social services is the 'guaranteed minimum' which means

> state guarantees a minimum supply of certain essential goods and serv-ices (such as medical attention and supplies, shelter and education) or a minimum money income available to be spent on essentials – as is the case of old age pensions, insurance benefits and family allowances (Marshall 1992 [1950], 32).

This emphasis on the centralised state within public services was part of a broader set of debates that presented a choice between the state and the market as the basic alternative when considering issues of public policy. Samuel Bowles and Herbert Gintis comment

> prejudices of conservative policy stem from its recognition of weaknesses in the state but not in the market as governance structures. The selective treatment leads to a view that the state is an arena of wasteful rent-seeking, while the market economy is efficient, a view from which exclusive reliance on the market ineluctably follows. Advocates of egalitarian economic policy, by contrast, while treating the market as riddled with co-ordination failures, have often failed to recognize the limitations of the state as an effective instrument for the implementation of economic objectives (Bowles and Gintis 1998, 9).

Towards the latter part of the twentieth century, the value of the state versus market dichotomy began to be increasingly called into question. Various commentators pointed out that the 'state versus market' framework provided a poor description of reality. A range of institutions from both the public and private realms were involved in issues of public policy, and these agencies were combined in different ways in different countries. The charge that state versus markets provided an inadequate description of reality also had a prescriptive dimension. It was hoped that by laying bare the complexities of the policy-making process, debates about public policy could go beyond the polemical dichotomy between states versus markets. The choices available to policy-makers were greater than a reliance on either the centralised state or free market.

The complexity of public policy is explored in a number of fields. One such area of study is comparative political economy. For example, Andrew Shonfield's (1965) *Modern Capitalism* explored the differences that exist within capitalism. Instead of trying to assess the strengths and weaknesses of capitalism as against communism, Shonfield sought to examine the variety that exists within capitalism. In his analysis Shonfield made a distinction between the use of planning within the version of capitalism in France with capitalist regimes elsewhere. Shonfield believed that the French experience provided a guide to how the problems inherent in capitalism can be tackled and overcome. Colin Crouch and Wolfgang Streeck observe that Shonfield's analysis found an audience keen to, 'hear of new ways that economies might be managed other than through the stereotypical alternatives of free markets and state ownership' (Crouch and Streeck 1997, ix). Shonfield is an early contributor to a variety of capitalism literature which explores different models of capitalism

(Goldthorpe 1984; Hall 1986; Albert 1993; Kitschelt et al. 1999; Coates 2000). Governance is another literature examining the complexity of public policy. The term gover*nance* is intended to highlight the role of a range of bodies besides central gover*nment* that is involved in the process of governing. Terms such as 'multi-level governance' have arisen to highlight the different levels or layers of governing (Gamble 2000; Scholte 2000; Bache and Flinders 2004). Perri 6, Diana Leat, Kimberley Seltzer and Gerry Stoker (2002) provide one such multi-level governance framework in their analysis of 'holistic governance'. Perri 6 and others argue that a variety of different agencies, both public and private, are likely to face many problems in common. These authors say that the thrust of the holistic approach is that it attempts to bring these different agencies together so that the solutions to these problems are joined-up rather than fragmented. They argue that the holistic approach is not opposed to policy specialisation but to policy fragmentation. Although these authors do not underestimate the scale of the task involved in securing holistic solutions, they reject a pessimistic view that joined-up solutions are impossible.

Although research conducted within comparative political economy and governance highlight the complexity of the policy process, the state versus market framework still has an important hold on how policy is discussed. Colin Crouch and Wolfgang Streeck (1997) comment that in some senses the state versus market framework had a firmer grip among policy-makers in the 1990s than the 1960s as free market or neoliberal ideas spread within international institutions. Colin Crouch and Wolfgang Streeck write that since 1992 an, 'uncritical neoliberalism has come to dominate thinking in many national governments as well as in international organizations' (Crouch and Streeck 1997, ix). Within public services, the opposition that discussing alternatives to centralisation tends to generate testifies to the associations that continue to exist between the centralised state and public services. Andrew Gamble and Will Paxton (2005) comment that, 'Whenever there are calls for the state to be made more democratic and accountable by encouraging greater decentralisation, the counter-argument always surfaces: that to do so risks making it less capable of delivering high quality and universal public services' (Gamble and Paxton 2005, 227–228).

There are grounds for rethinking public services, however, in ways that go beyond the options of the centralised state or free markets (Fung and Wright 2001; Corry and Stoker 2002; Gamble and Wright 2004). Archon Fung and Erik Olin Wright comment

As the tasks of the state have become more complex and the size of politics larger and more heterogeneous, the institutional forms of liberal democracy developed in the nineteenth century – representative democracy plus techno-bureaucratic administration – seem increasingly ill suited to the novel problems we face in the twenty-first century (Fung and Wright 2001, 5).

One might try to accommodate the challenges of public expectations, rising costs, New Right criticisms and globalisation through the centralised state. It is possible that centralisation may go some way towards meeting the above challenges. Exploring the other options that are available, however, is also an important task. Given that existing modes of thinking do not appear to have provided ready solutions to the problems highlighted above, there is a case for looking at alternatives to the centralised state and free markets.

This task of rethinking public services has already begun. An important part of this rethinking involves considering the role of choice within public services such as health and education (Ladd 2002; Hoxby 2003a, b; Lent and Arend 2004; Working Commission on Choice in K-12 Education 2004; Burgess et al. 2005). For example, in the United States, the Bill Gates Foundation and the Annie E. Casey Foundation established a national working commission based at the Brookings Institution in Washington, DC to investigate choice within K-12 level of education.[2] The Commission notes that choice has existed for some time within US education. The Commission says that six states have some form of state-funded voucher programme within schools (Colorado, Wisconsin, Florida, Vermont, Ohio and Maine) and three states have income-tax deductions for privately funded voucher schemes (Arizona, Florida and Pennsylvania). For example, in 1990, Wisconsin introduced a voucher policy to fund 1000 students in Milwaukee to attend private secular schools. In 1995, the programme was expanded to allow students to attend religious schools. The Milwaukee programme allows up to 15 per cent of students who attend the state system to attend private schools. Household size and income is used to calculate eligibility for the scheme. Household size is understood to cover all those who live in the household. For a two-person household, the qualifying income level is $21,460 per year. This figure is increased by $5,536 for each additional member of the household. More recently, the Commission notes that President George Bush introduced a No Left Behind Act in 2002 that bolstered choice within schools. This act requires school districts to provide choices for parents attending schools that consistently fail performance targets. In 2002–2003, more than 4800 of 93,000 schools across America failed such standards.

A related but different set of debates concentrates on how more participatory governance structures might be introduced within public services (Fung and Wright 2001, 2003; Mayo and Moore 2001; Crouch 2003; Wainwright 2003). These discussions focus on how public services can be moulded to allow the public a greater role or voice in managing and controlling their operations. For example, Archon Fung and Erik Olin Wright (2001) point to the use of participatory city budgeting in Porto Allegre in Brazil as an example of this approach. Fung and Wright note that Porto Allegre is the capital of Rio Grande do Sul, and has 1.3 million residents. In the late 1980s and early 1990s, a coalition of parties on the left gained control of the municipal government and introduced participatory budgeting. In each of the 16 regions that compose the city, a regional assembly meets twice a year to discuss budgetary issues. Although a variety of stakeholders can attend such meetings – including city executives, representatives of community organisations and administrators – only inhabitants of the region can vote in these sessions. These meetings are co-ordinated by individuals from the municipal government and community delegates. At the first meeting, officials from the municipal government report on the implementation of the previous year's budget. Delegates are then elected from those present at the assembly to investigate future priorities (such as land use, transportation and sewage). Those elected examine these areas in the three-month period before the next meeting. At the second meeting, the delegates report back and the assembly votes on spending proposals in the next year. Two delegates are then elected to represent the region at a citywide forum, which decides citywide budget out of these regional proposals. At the citywide forum, the regional delegates are joined by two elected delegates from each of the five thematic priorities representing the city as a whole – a delegate from the municipal workers' union, one from the union of neighbourhood associations and two from central municipal bodies. The council then decides the budget, which is ratified by the mayor. Fung and Wright note that in 1996 around 8 per cent of the residents of Porto Allegre attended the regional assemblies for the budget.

This rethinking arouses controversy. For example, a number of commentators are hostile to allowing choice within public services, fearing that it spells the possible break up and demise of public services (Crouch 2003; Marquand 2004). In its deliberations upon choice in the United States, the

Working Commission on Choice in K-12 Education reports that a
sober reflection of the desirability of choice is impeded by polemical
interventions by right and left alike. The Commission states that, 'At its
worst, the public debates about choice is partisan, shedding more heat than
light on the subject ... The debate about choice is too rarely what it should
be: a reasoned discussion of alternative arrangements for educating
children' (Working Commission on Choice in K-12 Education 2004, 15).
The Commission alleges that ideologues from the right insist that only markets
can support quality and fairness, while ideologues from the left contend that
market forces can only corrupt public purposes.

Although the task of rethinking public services is an important one, there
is considerable debate and controversy about the appropriate form public
services should take. Should choice be allowed within public services?
What role, if any, should the private sector play within public services?
Should user charges play any part in the funding of public services? What
follows is one attempt to consider some of the issues involved. In sum,
I present an argument for a 'participative' model of public services that
allows users to express both choice and voice within public services.

Implementing choice and voice suggest the need for a plural model of
public services that allows a role for a diverse range of providers. This
diversity allows a role for the private sector. Different providers should be
subject, however, to central regulation, and this points to a role for the state
and supra-state bodies. I do not suggest, however, that the same model of
public services will, or should, emerge everywhere. Although different
countries will have a common commitment to voice and choice, users and
public servants will engage with public services in different ways. No 'one-
size-fits-all' model will arise across different countries, and differences
exist between different countries.

My argument shares a common ground with a number of recent accounts
that go beyond a paternalistic view of public services in which users absorb
services from a class of professionals (Beauchamp and Childress 2001;
Coulter 2002; Le Grand 2003b). The emphasis on participation highlights
the fact that when thinking about public services one is not forced to go
down a centralising route. It is possible to envisage a different view in
which users might be more actively engaged. Much of the existing literature
on activity, though, tends to emphasise either voice or choice. For example,
Julian Le Grand's recent book *Motivation, Agency and Public Policy* is
heavily weighted to the exercise of choice. In contrast, interventions by figures such as Colin Crouch (2003) and David Marquand (2004) tend to
downgrade choice in favour of voice. My own view is that both these camps

contain insights and that a role for voice and choice should be explored as part of attempts to encourage participation. The nature of the argument I consider in relation to voice and choice rests on an engagement with knowledge-based arguments put forward by Friedrich Hayek. Although Hayek's arguments have been the subject of some debate (Miers 2003; Wainwright 2003), these contributions tend to either side with or reject Hayek's account. I try to combine insights from both these different approaches.

The argument in this book is shaped by a distinction between the values that public services are supposed to embody and the contingent means used to achieve these ends. This distinction between ends and means is a source of debate and disagreement (Commission on Public Private Partnerships 2001; Corrigan and Steele 2001; Redwood 2002). Paul Corrigan and Jane Steele (2001b) present evidence that suggests that the appropriate relationship between the ends and means of public services is often a source of confusion for the public. As part of their study in Britain they convened two focus groups with members of the public aged 18–40 and 40–70, and conducted face-to-face interviews with 1000 people who were taken from a random sample of the population. All were asked about what they thought made a public service public. Corrigan and Steele note

> most striking theme of all is one of inconsistency. People came back again and again to the idea that a public service involves public money and government authority, but were unable to fit this together with a belief that public services should benefit society (Corrigan and Steele 2001b, 3).

In other words, there was confusion over the appropriate link between means (in this case public money and government authority), ends (the benefits to society) and public services.

The relationship between means and ends may be modelled in a number of ways. One conception identifies public services with a particular set of tools or instruments. For example, services might be identified with state funding and provision (Redwood 2002). The problem with this approach is that no reference is contained within it to the objectives that public services exist to serve. What is ultimately important within public services are the values they try to attain, not the instruments that are used to achieve these ends (Commission on Public Private Partnerships 2001; Crosland 1985). While values may remain fairly fixed over time, the precise mechanisms used to achieve these values may alter over time, depending up the particular circumstances and environment.

Although linking public services to values might seem superficially attractive, one possible objection is that it is not easy to separate out ends and means as straightforwardly as this approach implies. Ends might be *dependent* on means. For example, certain versions of voice involve creating spaces in which users can interact and, through a process of discussion and deliberation, decide the objectives to be adopted by their local provider. The ends of public services here result from the particular means that are used within these services.

It is true in this case that the ends are influenced by the means, and so the line of demarcation between ends and means is not clear cut. While overlaps between ends and means ought to be acknowledged, it is still valuable to distinguish between ends and means. On the one hand, there are areas in which ends and means can be fairly easily distinguished. Whether a government-funded programme is paid for through immediate taxes or through government borrowing is unlikely to have a bearing on the nature of the public value captured by the service. On the other hand, in those areas where overlaps do exist, a distinction between ends and means can be brought into play in a related realm. A central authority might specify the objectives that public services need to satisfy, but devolve power and decision making to local users and producers about the best way of achieving these standards. This devolution can encompass a role for the sort of forms for discussion described above. As will be seen later the importance of guaranteeing that all individuals have access to a minimum level of standards means that there has to be a role for a central authority to set and regulate these goals. This implies a separation of ends from means.

In line with the distinction between ends and means, the starting point of my argument relates to the values that public services should embody. This is considered in Chapter 2, which looks at issues of citizenship. The concept of the public value or public interest is inextricably bound up with the concept of citizenship (Commission on Taxation and Citizenship 2000; Leys 2001; Marquand 2004). The version of citizenship adopted carries important implications for the nature of public services. For example, a model of citizenship that confines attention to civil and political rights points to a primary role for those agencies, such as the police and army, that help protect civil and political rights, and a small role for other services such as health and education (there may, for instance, be a role for citizenship education in order to ensure people understand and exercise their political rights). A version of citizenship that pays attention to individual agency as well as civil and political rights has a much more prominent role for health and education services. The first part of the chapter defends the idea of social citizenship against attacks from the New Right. Although the idea of social citizenship is still a worthy aim of public policy, it should be crafted to adapt to the sorts of challenges mentioned above. This involves citizenship being able to accommodate pressures associated with globalisation, user expectations and rising costs. Amartya Sen's notion of 'capabilities and functionings' is suggested as a possible way of negotiating these challenges. The capability approach focuses on the capacity of people to function. This capacity to function allows people to deal with the sort of pluralism engendered within society by globalisation. The capacity to function within public services could also act as a way of promoting civic participation which is one way of trying to address user dissatisfaction. Providing people with resources to allow function is not cheap, and I consider some of the ways that these services can be funded. I continue that the provision of resources also imposes various obligations on people, which links in with attempts to prompt civic participation.

Chapter 2 suggests that resources should be provided to people so that they are capable of acting both inside and outside public services. This emphasis on activity within public services leaves open, however, the precise form that user participation should take. Chapter 3 picks up and contemplates this issue. Participation can be exercised through two main channels (Hirschman 1970; Le Grand 2003b; Marquand 2004). First, users could be provided with a voice within public services. This means that users are furnished with opportunities to express their views within a particular provider, and these views have a bearing upon the decisions made by managers of these organisations. Second, users could exercise choice. One important way that choice can be shaped is by providing people with choices between different providers. One strategy for promoting participation is to emphasise the role of only one of the above channels for activity. An alternative position is to allow a role for both voice and choice. Chapter 3 provides a case for permitting this alternative approach. It does this through a critical examination of one of the New Right's most important critiques of the state. In particular, I consider Friedrich Hayek's critique of state planning. For Hayek, the widespread dispersal of knowledge throughout society undermines the effectiveness of central planning. Competition is important for helping co-ordinate this 'tacit' or practical knowledge. While this provides an argument for choice between providers, the notion that knowledge can be created as well as discovered means a role for voice. The discovery and creation of knowledge supports utilising both user choice and voice.

Chapter 4 extends this discussion and considers some of the important organisational features that should be in place to make choice and voice a reality. Overall, the picture of public services should be one with a range of different providers operating within a framework of centrally defined standards. A range of suppliers, which allows a role for bodies drawn from the private sector, will help ensure there is sufficient capacity in the system of provision for people to exercise choice. Voice will provide a spur to diversity, as different users and employees are likely to demand different things from their provider. To protect the standards of service experienced by both user and employees, there should be a set of standards governing quality of service and working conditions. These regulations should be set at both a national and global level.

Chapter 4 sets a model of public services that differs from 'centralised command and control'. Although the centre still plays a role in setting and regulating the standards experienced by users and employees, it does not aim to control the operation of providers. This points to a system that goes beyond traditional bureaucratic control. Instead, users play a more active role in holding providers to account. Chapter 5 looks at this in more detail, examining in particular the 'public interest company'. The public interest company provides an exemplary institutional embodiment of local autonomy and common standards. Chapter 5 uses the public interest company applied to health to provide a concrete illustration of some of the issues faced in making organisations responsive to their users, or more broadly, stakeholders.

Having presented a version of public services that is designed to allow users a choice and voice within public services, Chapter 6 considers some of the criticisms that might be levelled at this approach. Two broad sets of criticism are contemplated. First, worries about the impact of diversity on equality. Second, concerns about introducing choice within public services. Both criticisms are prominent in current discussions about public services. Although arguments cannot be settled conclusively without further evidence, the chapter aims to provide a preliminary defence of the approach set out here.

I do not pretend that I have all the answers or that I ask all the relevant questions here. An exhaustive theoretical study would have to canvass all the available options in the realm beyond a state-centred and free market approach, as well as the different versions that could be constructed of a state-centred and market-based approach. A comprehensive empirical examination would study all the different sectors of the public services (such as health, education and local government) and all the different policies that could be developed in these different areas. This is a very large task that is likely to be beyond the analysis of any one book and any single author. My more limited aim is to engage in an examination of the features of one particular alternative to a state-centred approach. Hopefully, this analysis can be used to yield a variety of propositions that can be tested in subsequent empirical work.

Second, the task of exploring the principles that ought to govern services is unlikely to be welcomed by everyone. Some may be concerned that this risks subjecting public services to the latest fad or fashionable set of thinking. On this view, public services have been a laboratory for successive waves of thinking, from the new public management to the social investment state. One should not upend public services yet again. One might continue that the best way of proceeding is to eschew such grand narratives and build from the 'bottom-up'. Lessons should be drawn instead from careful empirical analyses of particular schemes or existing practice. Although I think one should be sensitive how a theory is applied, and should not challenge an existing set of assumptions for its own sake, the attempt to outline a body of principles is a valuable one. Public services are subject to shifting challenges and circumstances, and it is right to consider how services can adapt to these changes. In some situations existing institutions can accommodate these changes. In others, however, a more fundamental rethinking is required. In response to the injunction to build from the ground up I contend that any such examination involves a consideration of principles, whether or not this is made explicit. Principles are invoked when selecting the data to be collected and making judgements about initiatives. For example, one might assess the impact of a specific scheme on equality, which means equality is a guiding assumption. Principles are inescapable, even in apparently small-scale empirical projects. I suggest, therefore, that delineating a set of assumptions is a worthy one. While this will not remove all policy dilemmas, a discussion of principles can spotlight the policy options or choices that are available.

Third, I focus on themes that ought to inform the organisation of public services rather than how these notions can be translated into a viable reform programme. The actual mechanics of reform raises a series of interesting and significant issues. Important questions concern what chain of events is best placed to implement a particular set of institutions and what should be the timing of such steps. Is it better to engage in a programme where initiatives are implemented in rapid succession or is a more gradual approach which allows specific measures time to bed down preferable? Although questions of public service *reform* are important, I confine myself to addressing the prior question of what public services should in general look like. The answer to this will provide a foundation from which an analysis for reform may build.

2 Citizenship

Introduction

In the first chapter I claimed that it is important to make a distinction between means and ends when thinking about the nature of public services. In particular, we should distinguish between the ends that public services aim to satisfy and the contingent means used to try and achieve these objectives. In line with this distinction, this chapter starts the task of rethinking public services by considering the ends that public services ought to satisfy. Examining the objectives or proper ends of public services raises the question of what is in the public interest. The public interest focuses on the rights and duties that accrue to members of the public, and these rights and duties are bound up with the issue of citizenship (Commission on Taxation and Citizenship 2000; Leys 2001; Marquand 2004). Accordingly, this chapter concentrates on the issue of citizenship. I do two main things during this examination. First, I outline a model based on individual capacity and responsibility. This model advocates that governing authorities ought to distribute resources so that people can develop the capacity to be or do a range of things. However, the duty of the government to provide individuals with sufficient resources so that they can develop various capacities imposes a reciprocal obligation on people to make use of these capacities. Second, I relate this model of citizenship to the challenges facing public services outlined in the previous chapter. In particular, I consider a model of capability and responsibility in light of the challenges posed by user expectations, rising costs, New Right criticisms and globalisation. I suggest that one of the attractions of a model of capability and responsibility is how it may help public services accommodate and cope with these issues.

Before progressing, a few comments are in order about the notion of the public interest. I have invoked the concept of the public interest when discussing the goals that public services have to achieve. However, some observers are sceptical about the idea of the public interest. In particular, the public choice wing of the New Right views the public interest as an empty concept that masks the reality of a clash of private interests. According to

25

public choice thought, individuals deploy resources in order to advance their private interests. Although these theorists accept that people refer to the public interest when attempting to shape public policy, this is viewed as a convenient fiction that allows people to further their own interests. Public choice thinkers wish to dispense with the notion of the public interest. Instead, public policy should be confined to setting out a framework within which people will pursue their private interests. Against this, while it is true that private interests play an important role in public policy, and that individuals or groups sometimes refer to the public interest in order to advance their own private interests, the concept of the public interest is not an empty one. Defining the framework in which individuals follow their private interests is itself a political question, and that the choices about the appropriate level of public intervention feeds unavoidably off a concept of the public interest. In other words, the notion of the public interest is embedded within the prescriptions made by public choice theorists. While the notion of the public interest that is implicit within the public choice critique is of course different from that advanced by others, it is still a recognisable model of the public interest. Public interest is not a concept devoid of content (Gamble 2000; Gamble and Kelly 2000).

Although the public interest is not an empty concept, it can be understood in different ways. Historically, the public interest has often been thought to possess a universal and objective character. On this conception, public interest refers to a set of principles that are the same throughout time and across different societies. This conception also had an elitist bias insofar as political elites were often thought to have special access to the universal definition of the public interest. The notion of pluralism used in this book, as well as the idea that non-elite groups possess knowledge, raises difficulties for using this notion of the public interest in this book. However, Andrew Gamble and Gavin Kelly point out that there is an alternative conception of the public interest that does not refer to a static set of truths but instead to a concept of the public interest that emerges from dialogue and discussion. More broadly, this links the public interest to politics. They note

> essential step which has to be taken is to develop the notion that the public interest arises through politics. Even if we accept that individuals and their interests are the driving forces of modern politics, there is no reason to treat those interests as only definable and knowable by the individuals themselves. Individuals are part of communities, and the roles, identities and characteristics they acquire and choose are the product of the history of those communities (Gamble and Kelly 2000, 25).

Different discussions in different communities will give rise to different conceptions of the public interest. Some users might prioritise cleanliness in the hospitals they attend; others might be more concerned about getting the appointment that would suit them. Instead of a single and universal model of the public interest, there is a plural concept of the public interest. This version of the public interest chimes more readily with the analysis of this book and is the understanding of the public interest that is deployed here.

Capability

The capability approach originates in the work of the Indian economist Amartya Sen (1984, 1985, 1999). This stimulates interest within the academy and the policy-world. Within the academy, the capability approach attracts the attention and is developed by researchers across the world, in places such as the United States (Nussbaum 2000, 2001; Sherraden 2003), Australia (Pettit 1999; Jayasuriya 2000) and Britain (Commission on Taxation and Citizenship 2000). At a policy-level, the capability approach helps inform the United Nation's Human Development Report. In 1990, the United Nations began to publish a series of annual reports charting the state of development across the world. These reports are available in more than 12 languages and launched in over 100 countries. These reports place human development at the heart of their analysis. Amartya Sen's capability approach is used to help construct and shape the indices used to measure human development (Callinicos 2000; Nussbaum 2001; Fukuda-Parr 2002).

The heart of the capability approach focuses on the capacity of individuals to perform various functions. Amartya Sen (1999) characterises capabilities as concentrating on an individual's 'beings' or 'doings', that is, what people are able to be or do. A 'functioning' is the building block or basic element of the capability approach. A functioning looks at a person's capacity to function in a particular area. A functioning is a specific instance of a person being able to be or do something. For example, a person could be healthy or be educated. A person's capability is a collection of all that a person is able to be or do, that is a collection of all their individual functionings.

Examples

Martha Nussbaum (2000, 2001) highlights the importance of ten functionings in her account of capability. First, being able to experience a life of normal length. This means that a person should not die prematurely. Second, to be able to have good health. This implies that individuals should have adequate food and shelter. Third, to have bodily integrity. This means that people should be able to move freely between locations without being subject to coercion or violence. Fourth, to be able to use their senses. This means that people should be able to think and reason. Individuals should be shaped by an adequate education and engage in freedom of expression. Fifth, to be able to form commitments to people or objects that are external to themselves. This is the ability to form emotions. Sixth, to be able to set out an individual conception of the good and follow one's plans. Seventh, to be able to engage in forms of human association, such as freedom of assembly and speech. Eighth, being able to have concern for the natural environment. Ninth, to be able to enjoy leisure activities. Tenth, being able to have control over one's political and material environment. This means being able to take part in political decision-making and having property rights on an equal basis with others.

The United Nations' 2005 Human Development Report deploys four indices to measure functionings and capabilities. First, a human development index that provides a general measure of human development. This presents a general summary of development towards three broad functionings: having a long and healthy life, knowledge and having a decent standard of living. Life expectancy at birth is used to help calculate an index measuring a long and healthy life. The adult literacy rate and the number of people enrolled within primary, secondary and tertiary education is used to measure knowledge. Gross domestic product per head of population is deployed to assess a decent standard of living. Second, a human poverty index is used to measure capability deprivations along the dimensions of a long and healthy life, knowledge and a decent standard of living. One index is created for developing countries, and one measure is used for countries in the Organization for Economic Co-operation and Development (the index for the latter countries also measures social exclusion, which is calculated from the long-term unemployment rate). Different methods are used to measure progress within the developing world and OECD. For example, in the former countries a decent standard of living is measured by the percentage of the population without a sustainable access to an improved water source and the percentage of children who are underweight for age, while in the latter countries standard of living is measured by the percentage of people below the poverty line. Third, a gender development index focuses on inequalities between men and women as regards a long and healthy life, knowledge and standard of living. The measures are constructed from male and female life expectancy at birth (for a long and healthy life), male and female literacy rates (for knowledge) and male and female earned income (for standard of living). Fourth, a gender empowerment measure examines differences between men and women in relation to economic and political participation. Political participation in decision-making is calculated from male and female shares of parliamentary seats. Economic participation in decision-making is determined from male and female shares of professional, technical, legislative, senior official and managerial posts. Power over economic resources is measured by male and female incomes (United Nations 2005).

Freedom

The capability approach provides the basis for a particular concept of freedom, combining elements of positive and negative freedom. Historically, two concepts have dominated thinking about freedom. Negative freedom conceives freedom in terms of absence from external restraint. This means that a person is not prevented from pursuing their personal plans by some outside body. Negative freedoms emphasise 'freedom from' restraint. Positive versions of freedom suggest that even though a person may not face external restraint, they may still be unable to pursue their personal goals through a lack of resources. They may lack the skills to get a job or not have enough money to pay for a training course. Although a variety of options may be formally available to the individual, they may not have the resources to pursue these options. Positive freedom provides resources to individuals so that they can realise their opportunities. They provide people with the 'freedom to' pursue their goals (Berlin 1958). Capabilities aim to expand the range of choices available to individuals. This tries to ease the restrictions placed on choice and so connects with negative freedom. However, the capability perspective intersects with positive freedom by ensuring that people have the capability to exercise choice. Kanishka Jayasuriya comments that, 'real freedom to choose (a form of negative freedom) needs a dose of positive freedom in order to enable individuals to achieve certain kinds of capability' (Jayasuriya 2000, 290).

The capability approach supports providing resources to individuals to allow them to develop functionings. Some people may require a greater share of resources than others, however, to develop a particular state of being or doing. For example, a person with physical disabilities may need a larger share of resources than a person without such disabilities to attain a given level of health. Supporting the equality of capability between different people means distributing a larger share of resources to the person with disabilities. This will allow everyone to enjoy a comparable level of health. Although capabilities require resources, implementing equality of capabilities allows resources to be distributed unequally between different individuals. On this matter, the capability approach is set against two other influential accounts for distributing resources (Callinicos 2000; Fukuda-Parr 2002). First, a capability standpoint is opposed to utilitarianism. According to utilitarianism, the best act is that which maximises the total sum of utility across a society. Utilitarianism is composed of three basic components. The first of these is the belief that all actions must be judged by the consequences or results they create. The second element judges states of affairs in terms of the utility they produce, understood broadly to cover the happiness generated for different people. The third aspect says that aggregate merit is determined by the sum of utilities that are generated. Utilitarianism possesses a number of strengths. These include the importance of using results to help judge social arrangements, and the attention paid to happiness as a component of individual well-being. In spite of this, utilitarianism also suffers from important weaknesses. Utilitarianism focuses only on maximisation of utility, not how utility is distributed across society. However, since utility is an important part of a person's well being, guaranteeing well being for all individuals across society means that any assessment of different states of affairs has to contemplate how utility is spread across a population. Also, while utility can provide useful information about a person's well being, it can at times be unreliable. This occurs in situations where individuals adapt their preferences to reflect the constraints they face. The fact that individuals learn to take great pleasure for small mercies should not make this situation desirable. Utilitarianism, moreover, ignores non-utility pieces of information that are important for judging individual well-being. A person's health and educational status are also valuable indicators. These shortcomings mean that there is a need to go beyond utilitarianism (Sen 1999).

Second, a capability approach is set against a primary goods perspective. This theory states that all individuals should have access to a certain number of primary goods or resources that are deemed important for a valuable life. Although the primary goods stance is to be commended for taking into account the inequalities that arise between different people as well as the importance of non-utility indicators such as health and education, it suffers from the drawback that it does not consider the way people are able to 'convert' the primary goods received. Some people may require a greater share of resources in order to meet some minimum prescribed quality of life because they face greater difficulties than others do in converting these primary goods into something worthwhile. Sen comments that it is important to take account 'not only of the primary goods that persons respectively hold, but also that of the relevant personal characteristics that govern the *conversion* of primary goods into the person's ability to promote her ends' (Sen 1999, 74).

Responsibility

The capability approach supports providing people with resources so that they can develop the capacities to do or be something. If people are to do a particular thing, however, they must be both able and willing to do that thing. It is not enough to focus on an ability to perform a task, it is also important to look at a person's motivations to execute a function. The capability approach raises issues of individual motivations, and this in turn connects with the question of personal responsibility. Amartya Sen writes that, 'having the freedom and capability to do something does impose on the person the duty to consider whether to do it or not, and this does involve individual responsibility. In this sense, freedom is both necessary and sufficient for responsibility' (Sen 1999, 284).

The capability perspective imposes an obligation on governing authorities to ensure that people have sufficient resources to achieve various functionings. There are grounds for believing that if people are supplied with resources from governing agencies, then individuals have a corresponding obligation to make use of these resources (Marquand 1997; White 2003; Miller 2005). David Marquand argues that, 'If social rights are to be justified on grounds of agency, should not agents act? If resources are redistributed in your favour, are you not under some obligation to make proper use of them?' (Marquand 1997, 43). Stuart White (1997, 2000, 2003) argues that individual responsibility is justified on the grounds of fair reciprocity. In particular, if a person is willing to partake in the benefits produced by a society, but does not play any relevant part in the production of those benefits, then they are guilty of free-riding on those that do make such a contribution. In this case, the person is willing to share the benefits but not the costs of social co-operation. White contends that an individual who does not play a role commits a form of exploitation on those that do play a role, and tackling this exploitation is a proper concern of justice. He says that a principle of reciprocity requires that those who receive resources should have reciprocal obligations to execute. White says that reciprocity may be shaped in a number of ways, and he favours a 'fair dues' conception that relates duty to the ability to perform the obligation. White suggests that some people may be better placed at carrying out obligations than others. He states a system in which contributions are strictly proportional to the benefits received would impose a larger burden on those who are less able to perform the duty. A fairer system would connect responsibility to the capacity to perform the obligation. White says that similar sentiment informs Karl Marx's injunction that 'from each according to their ability, to each according to their needs'. White says that the notion of *fair* reciprocity means that while governing authorities are right to highlight the role of reciprocal obligations, fairness dictates that governing agencies should make available adequate and sufficient resources to individuals in the first place. Thus, the obligations of individuals rest on the obligations of governing bodies to provide people with sufficiently generous material resources.

The principle of reciprocity provides one rationale for what has been called 'welfare contractualism', that is balancing rights with responsibilities (Giddens 1998, 2000; White 2000). The rights of individuals to material resources are matched by a set of reciprocal duties. One of the most prominent contemporary expressions of this type of welfare is 'workfare' schemes in the United States and Western Europe (King and Wickham-Jones 1999; White 2003; Handler 2004). Joel Handler argues that in the United States the idea of rights and responsibilities informs the Personal Responsibility and Work Opportunity Reconciliation Act introduced by President Bill Clinton in 1996. This Act links the receipt of welfare payments with the duty to seek work. Work requirements are enforced through financial penalties and time limits. States are mandated to reduce payments to those individuals who refuse to take part in work or work-related activities. Welfare assistance is restricted to a maximum of two consecutive years with a five-year limit imposed over a person's lifetime. Part of the Act also focuses on 'family values'. For instance, the Act stops payments going to parents under 18 years of age who are not engaged in educational activities or living with an older person in a supervised environment (Handler 2004). In Europe, the Swedish Parliament passed in 1998 the Responsibility of the Municipalities Act for Young People between 20 and 24 Years Old. This Act notes that during the first 90 days of unemployment, local labour offices are in charge of the young unemployed. Once the 90 days have elapsed, young people would become the responsibility of the municipality and would be offered a place on a municipal work scheme or take part in a training programme for up to one year. Young people are obliged to accept any offer or risk losing benefit. Similarly, in Denmark measures to tackle unemployment for low-skilled people under 25 years old means that after being unemployment for six months these young people had a 'right and duty' to education or work-training for at least 18 months. In the period after the six months, these young people would be on reduced benefits. From 1999, these measures were introduced for all people in this age group. Those who had formal qualifications have a right and duty to activation before the end of the six-month period (Kildal 2001).

Contract or virtue?

The above invokes the notion of contract in the discussion of responsibility. A contract helps capture the rights and responsibilities associated with citizenship. Some commentators question, however, whether it is appropriate to use contracts to help capture responsibility. For example, Andrew Dobson (2004) argues that at the heart of contracts is the notion of exchange, whereby each contacting party agrees to provide a good or service to the other partners in exchange for another good or service. This exchange is backed up by a system of threats and punishments if the various agreements are not carried out. Dobson sees contracts as belonging to the economic sphere and not to citizenship. He writes that the, 'language of contract does not mark off citizenship as a special and distinct kind of relationship but, rather, associates it closely with the juridical–economic sphere and the expectations and assumptions that lie therein' (Dobson 2004, 46). He says that seeing responsibility in terms of contract presents two problems. First, contracts can have perverse effects. He gives the example of a recycling scheme whereby a local council was proposing to charge people for taking over-quota sacks of rubbish away. He says that the problem with this idea is that people will have an incentive to dump their extra sacks of rubbish elsewhere (neighbour's yards, fields and so on) in order to avoid paying the charges. Second, he argues that even for those contracts that can be well designed, responsibility will evaporate once contracts are removed. This is problematic because while responsibility is indeed important, contracts are subject to the vagaries of political fashion. If a government of a different political stripe chooses to abolish the contracts established by its predecessor, then the roots of responsibility can be easily removed. In order to place responsibility on a more secure footing, Dobson argues for a remoralisation of politics that places individual virtue at the heart of responsibility. Virtue refers to individual excellencies such as care and compassion, and for Dobson this provides the basis for obligation.

Although Dobson makes an important case for virtue as a component of responsibility, several things can be said in response to his critique. First, contracts do not belong solely in the economic realm. Although contracts are an important part of the economic sphere, contracts are also a staple of the political realm. Versions of the 'social contract' can be detected in a long lineage of thinkers, from Jean-Jacques Rousseau to John Rawls. Arguably contracts are just as much part of politics as they are of economics and accordingly should not be seen simply as an economic device. Second, contracts can be defended as a matter of justice. The above analysis highlights the role of reciprocity as a principle of justice. An emphasis on reciprocity provides a rationale for contract. Thus, even if one wishes to have a role for virtue, there is a case for allowing a role for contract in attempts to foster responsibility. This connects to a broader point that virtue and contract are not mutually exclusive, and it is possible to develop both when trying to foster responsibility.

Third, it is true that contracts can have perverse consequences. Rather than abandoning contracts we might try to see whether they can be better designed. Of course, problems may remain. However, it may be possible to overcome difficulties, and indeed in some situations the issue of perverse results may not arise. One way of reducing the difficulties associated with devising contracts is to write contracts that work with the grain of human motivations. This reduces the likelihood of counterproductive results. There are grounds for suspecting that most people are driven by a mix of 'knavish' and 'knightly' motives (Birchall and Simmons 2002; Le Grand 2003b). Knaves focus on the most effective way of deploying the resources at their disposal in a way that maximises their self-interest. Knights act out of noble non-self-interested reasons. One way of fashioning policy in a society in which people are both knights and knaves is to implement measures only on the assumption that knavish motivations dominate. The logic behind this is that the knaves' strategy seems safest because it will be well-suited to a situation where people are actually knaves. If people are actually knights, then individuals will avoid triggering off the mechanisms designed to channel knavish behaviour to the common good because they are motivated by an ethic of service. This approach assumes that the motivations of knights will be unaffected by the knaves' strategy. However, there is evidence to suggest that this strategy can help turn knights into knaves (Titmuss 1971; Frey and Oberholzer-Gee 1997). This turning of knights into knaves is problematic because it can make a policy of fostering responsibility more difficult and costly than relying on both knightly and knavish motivations. For example, Bruno Frey and Felix Oberholzer-Gee (1997) examined the use of monetary incentives to persuade members of local communities in Switzerland to accept a nuclear waste plant in their area. More than three hundred people were surveyed in their study. At first, there was no suggestion that local residents would be offered any monetary rewards for accepting a plant in their neighbourhood. More than half (51 per cent) of the people surveyed supported locating the plant in their area. The question was then repeated, with the promise that the government would provide compensation to residents if they accepted the plant. Different amounts were offered to different groups (of up to 12 per cent of Swiss median income). It was found that monetary rewards reduced public support for the plant by more than half (to 25 per cent). The researchers found this reduction was not due to any changed perception of the risks involved with the plant. A knavish strategy of emphasising the role of monetary incentives appeared to alter the way that a number of the population addressed the issue. Some who were inclined to respond in a knightly fashion now seemed to approach the issue in a knavish frame of mind. The incentives offered now were not sufficient for a proportion of these people to accept a plant in their neighbourhood.

A different strategy is to advance proposals that are consonant with both knightly and knavish motivations. This avoids one having to commit to one type of motivational structure and so appeal to the range of motivations found within society. Julian Le Grand advances partnership schemes as an example of this approach. He says that there is a significant probability that persons over the age of 65 will require long-term residential care. Le Grand argues that the provision of such care is expensive, and it would be very costly for government to meet all of the costs. He says that there is a case for government providing a basic, but adequate, level of service for all. However, any additional expenditure should be met through a partnership between individuals and government. He says that a matching scheme could be put in operation in which people who saved for their long-term care could attract a matching contribution from government (the government's matching funds would be capped at a certain level). On the one hand, this would appeal to self-interest by providing people with an incentive to save. On the other hand, it would appeal to peoples' sense of fairness, insofar that those people who exercise responsibility and save would impose a recipro-cal obligation on government. The partnership scheme is an instance of the contractual approach and shows how contracts can be used to adapt to both knavish and knightly motivations. While it should be admitted that it is not always easy to reconcile knightly and knavish motivations, there do seem to be important areas in which policy can be devised to provide robust incentives.

Challenges

I have set out above the model of citizenship that informs the analysis of this book. I now consider this view of citizenship in light of the challenges facing public services discussed in the previous chapter. Although a model of capability and responsibility can be justified in ways that are not connected to public services, one of the attractions of this version of citizenship is that it constitutes a potential way of addressing the challenges mapped out in the introductory chapter. The capability and responsibility approach is most relevant in terms of the challenges posed by user expectations and globalisation. Although capability and responsibility offers less in relation to rising costs and New Right critique over other models of social citizenship, it nevertheless has the potential to accommodate both of these issues.

User expectations

In the introductory chapter, I noted the challenge posed to public services by user expectations. One way of trying to address user expectations is to promote user involvement in public services. The idea here is that involving users within public services creates an opportunity for users to shape or influence the services they experience (Mayo and Moore 2001; Coulter 2002; Chen 2003; Le Grand 2003b). Angela Coulter comments

> public expectations are changing and ... clinical practice and the organi-
> sation of health care delivery must change too. A more active role for the
> patient and greater public management in health policy-making could help
> ensure more appropriate treatment and care, improve health outcomes,
> reduce errors and improve safety, reduce complaints and litigation, raise
> quality standards, and improve accountability, public understanding and
> social solidarity (2002, 106).

Of course, user involvement is not without problems. It may not be easy to encourage users to participate within public services (an issue taken up in Chapter 5). Even if users are involved, this participation might not translate into influence if their views are ignored. Although the scope for user involvement as a way of addressing rising expectations should not be exaggerated, it seems unlikely that public services will be able to engage with rising expectations without some form of user involvement.

The capability approach can help address user expectations by providing people with the capacities needed to be involved in public services. User involvement can be conducted through one of two main channels (Hirschman 1970; Le Grand 2003b; Marquand 2004). First, users can exercise 'voice'. This occurs when those dissatisfied with the performance of an organisation express their concerns to managers. Executives may be made aware of issues they did not previously recognise, or pressure is brought to bear on things that managers did recognise but ignored. Managers then take remedial action designed to address these shortcomings. Second, users may 'exit'. Exit involves a person who is dissatisfied with an organisation from leaving that body. This puts pressure on managers to stem decline in order to prevent further people from quitting and threatening the viability of the organisation.

Albert Hirschman argues that voice and exit offer opposing routes for stemming decline. While voice encourages people to stay and fight their corner, exit provides an opportunity for them to quit. Although these are opposing strategies, Hirschman recognises that it is possible that one strategy can enhance the other. Managers of failing organisations may be tempted to sideline or ignore user voice if there is no threat that dissatisfied individuals will leave the organisation. Voice might be reduced to a talking shop. Albert Hirschman says

chances for voice to function effectively as a recuperation mechanism are appreciably strengthened if voice is backed up by the *threat of exit*, whether it is made openly or whether the possibility of exit is merely well understood to be an element in the situation by all concerned (Hirschman 1970, 82).

Although this suggests that it is useful to combine voice and exit, it is possible to try and separate voice and exit and only endorse one route for citizen participation. The issue of what form participation should take will be examined in more depth in the next chapter, when I put forward a case for combining voice and exit.

Individuals need various capacities in order to be able to exercise voice and exit effectively. The capability approach can assist by providing people with the resources needed for voice and exit. For example, education is likely to be important for the exercise of voice and exit. In order that people are able to conduct voice or exit on an informed basis, they require data on the performance of an organisation. People need to be able, however, to understand and process this information. The capability approach can provide people with the skills to sift through and process this data. In addition to these basic processing and analytical capacities, voice requires that people are able to engage in reasoned discussion and debate. They need skills to conduct discussions with others, reflect on the arguments put forward in these debates and revise opinions as appropriate. The capability approach can provide a foundation for the acquisition of these skills. This view of citizenship can also help people acquire the other resources they need to participate within public services. For instance, people may need financial resources to pay for childcare that will allow them to attend meetings within schools or hospitals. People also need a modicum of good health if they are to play an active role within public services. Capabilities can help in all of these matters.

Globalisation

Perhaps the main challenge globalisation poses public services relates to the creation of a more complex society. Complexity exists at a variety of levels, and for our purposes, it is sufficient to note complexity at the level of personal goals and at the realm of personal circumstances. The first type of complexity refers to the different goods that people want their public services to satisfy. Users have probably always agreed that above all they want their local school or hospital to deliver a good service. The question that arises from this is what exactly constitutes a 'good' service. How do people value and prioritise issues such as efficiency, responsiveness, usability and accountability? In a fairly homogeneous society, people will adopt a similar understanding of what comprises a good service. In a more differentiated society, the answer to the above question will become more varied. Under globalisation, the range of things that people value in their services are increasingly differentiated. This pluralism of personal goals is arguably not only a fact, but also a value. 'Moral pluralism' suggests that there is no single vision of the good life and that the good can be conceived in a variety of ways.

The second type of complexity refers to the increased diversity of the personal circumstances of people within society. Diversity of circumstances has always been a feature of society. While differences have always been important, they are more intense today. For example, changes in the pattern of employment and moves towards 'post-industrial' society have contributed to the diversity of personal circumstances. Within industrial society, production was often organised on a large-scale basis. Large numbers of people operated in similar working conditions. These class experiences were broken up as large-scale economic activity began to be replaced by smaller-scale production (driven by consumer demand, for example, for more diversified products). Different working experiences began to proliferate from this, deepening differences in circumstances (Jayasuriya 2000).

Although the capability approach points to a model of citizenship where different individuals hold important things in common, it also lays the basis for a differentiated model of citizenship. This differentiation occurs because different people can be provided with resources in order to develop different functionings (and hence different capability sets). People can acquire different functionings in order to satisfy both the different goals that people value and the different circumstances that they find themselves in. The way that the capability approach has already been applied to promote the agency of women provides an indication of the way that this approach can adapt to complex society. One of the most telling criticisms of the way that citizenship was conceived within the post-war welfare state is that this failed to take proper account of the specific challenges faced by women. In particular, much of the welfare state was based on a 'male breadwinner' model in which men would be in full-time stable employment while their wives would be at home looking after the children. A feminist critique charged that model with ignoring the extent that male employment – and more generally the participation of men in the public realm – was based on the subjection of women within the family. Men could only enjoy the lifestyles they pursued if their female partners performed the bulk of domestic tasks. Feminists highlighted the 'gendered' nature of citizenship, and the consequent need to reconstruct citizenship so that it addresses the everyday experiences of women (Lister 1997; Dobson 2004). The capability approach is committed to developing the capacities of all individuals, regardless of gender. It recognises, however, that some people may need more resources than others to develop a comparable level of capabilities. In recognition of the discrimination faced by many women, the capability approach supports providing extra resources to women in order to correct for imbalances between the genders. For example, Jean Drèze and Amartya Sen (1997) argue that across much of India women exhibit lower levels of literacy than men. This gender imbalance matters because low literacy feeds into other inequalities that are harmful for the well-being of women. They argue that there is a case for measures to promote female education in order to tackle this gender inequality in literacy. The sensitivity shown to women is an example of a broader sensitivity to personal circumstances.

Rising costs

Promoting the development of individual capacity is not cheap. For example, health and education are likely to be important for any set of functionings (Drèze and Sen 1997; Jayasuriya 2000). Paying for the health and education services that support healthy and educated citizens will require substantial sums of money. There are grounds for believing that these costs are rising. Chapter 1 mentioned the upward pressure placed on health costs by developments in medical technology. Within education, global economic changes are placing an increasing premium on skills. For example, skills help people manage change by assisting people move more easily between different jobs as the 'job for life' declines. An emphasis on skills provides a case for expanding higher education and this expansion carries significant implications for cost (Barr 2001).

Government taxes will be crucial to any system of funding. Not everyone will be in a position to pay for the services they need. Individuals may, for example, be in jobs that do not pay sufficiently well and do not have access to assets that can offset any shortfall. These individuals have little option but to rely on a redistribution of income from the better-off if their needs are to be met. While charitable donations may provide a basis for some of the funds that the needy require, it is unlikely that voluntary redistribution will be enough to guarantee that everyone will have access at all times to the resources they rely on. Some form of compulsory redistribution is likely to be necessary. The state is probably the only agent within a nation that is capable of carrying out such a task.

There are also efficiency arguments for state funding. Tim Jenkinson (2003) argues that state finance possesses important advantages over private funding of public services. He contends that complexity is a hallmark of public services. He says that complexity arises because of the multiple objectives that public services have to serve, as well as the different constituencies that public services have to attend. According to Jenkinson, within the public realm, the nature of the relationships that exist between different providers is largely informal and implicit and that the relationships are handled on the basis of trust. In contrast, the private sector relies on explicit contracts to define and mediate all relationships. Jenkinson argues that there are lower contracting costs associated with the public realm than the private sector. The implicit nature of contracts in the public realm avoids the costs connected with explicit contracts (in terms of lawyers' fees, monitoring costs and so on). Of course, we can qualify the above arguments. For example, explicit contracts do not necessarily define the public realm.

Explicit contracts – such as Public Service Agreements which arise when the finance ministry provides money in exchange for public agencies agreeing to use these funds to meet set goals – can be developed in the public sphere. Similarly, implicit or 'relational' contracts can be developed in private corporations (Kay 1996). While the efficiency gains relying on state funding can be overstated, it is likely that there is an efficiency case for using state funding. The above arguments apply to any model of citizenship, not just the capability approach. Although the public funding of citizenship is not specific to the capability approach, the capability perspective has an impact on the character of public intervention. For example, the capability approach provides a rationale for progressive taxation, that is taxing those on high incomes more heavily than those on low incomes. Those on high incomes have a greater capacity to pay taxes than others. Respecting an 'equality of sacrifice' from different individuals implies that the rich should have to pay more taxes than the poor (Commission on Taxation and Citizenship 2000). The capability approach also supports moves towards enhancing financial autonomy, that is the choices individuals can make over financial matters. Supporting financial autonomy means that individuals should be the basis of the tax and benefit system rather than the household. This approach accords equal status to different members of the household. Women experience therefore the same rights as men within the household. The capability approach ensures that citizenship reaches down to the private realm of the family and is not simply focused on the public realm.

Although government taxes form a central plank in funding arrangements for public services, taxes alone are unlikely to be sufficient to pay for all rises in cost. If government taxes are the sole source of funding for public services, then taxes will have to rise, in some cases substantially, in order to cover rising costs. Although doubt is cast in Chapter 1 on the idea that global economic changes have removed the capacity of government to raise additional taxes this does not mean that there do not exist important constraints on raising taxes. The public is likely to exhibit resistance to the imposition of additional taxes, particularly where there exists dissatisfaction with the state of public services. While the global economy has not undermined the capacity of government to raise taxes, national politics may make this a difficult option to pursue. This limits the ability of government to rely simply on the public purse to pay for costs. This means that other sources of funding will be needed to help meet costs. The main options are the imposition of user charges or money from other organisations. The next chapter points to a useful role that may be allowed for funds from private organisations within public services. Here I look at the role of user charges or 'co-payment'. This means that users will have to pay a fee for a service over and above the taxes they pay. They may pay for this immediately at the point of delivery, or payments may be deferred. User charges cover things such as congestion charges for road use, tuition fees for higher education or prescription charges for drugs or medicines.

The view that user charges might serve citizenship is not a new idea. For example, in *The Future of Socialism* Anthony Crosland argues that user charges can help advance citizenship if they help ensure that public services deliver comparable levels of service to that experienced in the private sector. Crosland argues that social equality – where different individuals enjoy an equality of status – is an important aspect of citizenship. He contends that while social equality supports the universal availability of services, it need not entail the free availability of services. He says that what is important in overcoming the social distinctions that the rich enjoy over the poor is for individuals to have access to a broadly similar level of service, not whether they are necessarily free. He argues that social differentiation is more likely to arise from a situation where rich people can opt out of public provision to enjoy a much higher level of service in the private sector than in a situation where modest charges are imposed and the funds raised are used to help ensure that the public sector delivers services that are not of less quality than those experienced in the private sector. In terms of the model of citizenship set out above, an emphasis on reciprocity can provide a case for individuals providing a financial contribution through the payment of a user fee. The reciprocal nature of the obligation is intended to highlight that individuals contribute financially in response to a monetary contribution from governing authorities. In a situation in which tax receipts do not cover the full costs of a service, individual responsibility can play a role in furnishing a rationale for individuals to make a contribution to address a fiscal shortfall.

Tuition fees for students in higher education provides an example of how user fees might work in practice. Nicholas Barr (2001) sets out a scheme for funding an expansion of higher education that involves user fees for students. Under his scheme, in addition to funds received from government taxes each university would be able to charge tuition fees for their courses. Different fees could be set for different courses. Students would take out a loan from a student loans organisation and would pay back the loan after they leave university. Payments would be dependent on the income the person enjoys after leaving university and would be used to pay for the fees incurred during their study. Higher incomes would attract higher payments, and no payments would be made below a certain income level. In order to help address concerns over access for students from poorer backgrounds, Barr proposes that grant payments from both the government and universities (from the tuition fees they collect) would be offered to these students. Barr outlines the role of a mixed system of funding, with money coming from the state, individuals and universities.

Nicholas Barr argues that his proposals share important similarities to the system that is in place in the United States. Although Barr is not an uncritical admirer of the United States, he claims that the way of funding higher education in this country gets things broadly right. Barr says that higher education in the United States is arguably the largest and most diverse in the world. Using data drawn from the Organization for Economic Co-operation and Development for 1995, he says a greater percentage of gross domestic product is spent on higher education in the United States than in any other country in the Organization for Economic Co-operation and Development. The United States spends 2 per cent of its gross domestic product on higher education, its closest rivals being Sweden at 1.7 per cent (though this figure covers all of tertiary education), Australia at 1.5 per cent and Finland and the Netherlands at 1.3 per cent. Barr continues that there are multiple providers in the United States with around 3600 higher education institutions (1600 public and 2000 private providers) by the mid-1990s. In terms of funding, 60 per cent of funds for the system in the United States comes from non-governmental sources. In the mid-1990s, tuition fees provided roughly 27 per cent of the income of all universities. Variable fees are set by universities, though state universities are subject to some regulation. Students have access to mortgage type loans that help pay fees. Students agree to make repayments over a fixed number of years, with the repayments and payback period fixed at the time the loan is taken out. Barr opines that although mortgage type loans have advantages, such as the fact that the loan is transparent to students, they have various drawbacks. He says that uncertainty about the value of a qualification may deter some people from taking out a mortgage type loan. This may lead to underinvestment in higher education. He says that a loan of the sort he endorses avoids this problem because people will only start paying back the loan once their income reaches a certain level after they left university or college.

The idea of imposing user charges provokes concern and controversy (Crouch 2003; Lent and Arend 2004). Some commentators caution against presenting user charges as a way of raising revenue. For instance, Peter Robinson (2004) contends that the primary rationale for user charges should not be as a way of raising revenue but rather focus on the manner in which charges could help improve the quality of a service. For example, user fees on the roads could be justified on the basis that by encouraging people to avoid unnecessary journeys, these charges will help improve the quality of the good enjoyed by road-users (in terms, for example, of reduced travelling times to work). Robinson argues that a danger of emphasising revenue raising arguments is that it is not clear whether user charges are preferable to relying on additional taxes. Although Robinson is right in pointing out that a case should be made for linking the imposition of user charges with improvements in public services, the rising costs that public services face suggest that revenue arguments cannot be ignored entirely. User fees could be valuable on a revenue front if it were easier to raise extra funds through charges for certain areas of service rather than generalised tax increases.

Others worry about the impact of user charges on access to a service, fearing for example that students from poorer backgrounds will be deterred from going to university by the presence of tuition fees (indeed in some cases – as in road-pricing – the purpose of a charge is to reduce use of a service). Evidence exists which provides backing to the idea that co-payment can reduce use of a good. Carl Irvine and David Gratzer (2002) report that one of the largest and most wide-ranging tests of the impact of user fees on the behaviour of patients and healthcare outcomes in the United States ran from 1974 to 1982 and involved around 2000 non-elderly families and around 5800 individuals. Participants were offered either a free-care package or a user-fee plan. Irvine and Gratzer note that this study found that user-fee individuals made on average 47 per cent fewer visits for cases deemed less urgent that those who had to pay charges. Individuals who faced user fees also made 23 per cent fewer Emergency Room (ER) trips than those who did not have charges did. Moreover, only modest fees were needed to have such effects (though there were no significant differences in the health outcomes or satisfaction with health services between the user-fee or no-fee individuals).

Although access is a legitimate concern, this does not destroy the case for user charges. Steps can be taken to mitigate the effects of fees on access. Anthony Crosland suggests that fees should not be set for core areas where concerns over access are greatest. Moreover, fees should be restricted to modest levels. Although defining a core area is not an easy matter, this is not a hopeless task. Crosland identified health as one of the areas in which concerns about access are the greatest. Although there are arguably many aspects of health that can be described as core services, it is possible to develop systems of co-payment. Peter Robinson (2004) notes that in Sweden patients pay for various aspects of health care, with fees being set by local councils. For instance, in 2003 in Stockholm users paid 60 Swedish Kronas (around 6 Euros) for a visit to a dental hygienist, 240 Swedish Kronas (23 Euros) for a visit to casualty and 80 Swedish Kronas (roughly 8 Euros) per day for a hospital bed. A limit is set so that no one pays over 900 Swedish Kronas (around 87 Euros) for these charges over a year. Patients also pay an average of 25–30 per cent of the costs of prescription drugs, with their contributions capped at 1800 Swedish Kronas (approximately 175 Euros) over a period of a year. Exemptions from charges exist for particular demographic groups, such as children and young people. Although there is room for debate about whether these charges represent the best model of user charges, it seems possible to devise and implement a reasonable system of co-payment. Nicholas Barr (2001) describes above a system of higher education funding that combines student tuition fees with targeted help for students from poorer backgrounds. Barr notes that in terms of access participation rates in the United States are high. In 1994, 62 per cent of high school graduates went on to tertiary education (with 22 per cent doing two year courses and 40 per cent doing four year courses). Ultimately, we ought to recognise that co-payment can bring both advantages and disadvantages for citizenship. Rather than simply rule out user charges on the basis of the existence of negative effects, there is a case for trying to balance out these advantages and disadvantages. This stance allows a role for co-payment in public services.

New Right

In the introductory chapter I noted that the New Right is hostile to the notion of social citizenship. As the capability approach is an example of social citizenship, New Right thinkers will be opposed to this version of citizenship. In this section I address these criticisms of social citizenship. In particular, I focus on arguments put forward by Friedrich Hayek, who is the most significant thinker of the New Right. He outlines the most forceful criticisms of social citizenship from a New Right perspective (Tomlinson 1990; Harris 1998). I consider and reject his criticisms of social citizenship. This means that a model of capability and responsibility is robust to a New Right critique.

Friedrich Hayek makes several criticisms of social citizenship. Hayek argues that freedom simply refers to the 'state in which a man is not subject to coercion by the arbitrary will of another or others' (Hayek 1960, 11). Hayek says that this negative conception is the original view of freedom.

However, this conception became corrupted as liberty began to 'describe the physical "ability to do what I want," the power to satisfy our wishes, or the extent of the choice of alternatives open to us' (Hayek 1960, 16). Hayek continues that this positive notion confuses freedom with a different concept of ability. In particular, what this concept refers to here is the power of a person to meet their desires. He claims, however, that this is not the same as freedom, which is simply the absence of restraint. He argues that it is possible for someone to have the ability to pursue some opportunity but is not free to do this because he or she is restrained from doing so by outside interference.

In addition, Hayek attacks the concept of social justice that underpins positive freedom. On the one hand, Hayek feels that only intentional actions or foreseeable consequences should be a matter of justice. It is people's motives and intentions and foreseen consequences that are important when contemplating issues of justice. Intervening in markets in the name of social justice is not justified. Outcomes within markets are the unintended consequences of actions by individuals pursuing their own private ends. Hayek accepts that inequality is likely to arise in a market. While he says that inequality may be unfortunate, as it is not the result of intentional actions it is not a matter of justice (Hayek 1998 [1976]). On the other hand, he argues that even if the idea of social justice were seen as coherent in principle, trying to fashion a concept of social justice in practice would be a recipe for disaster. In particular, he argues that different people value different ends. He suggests that it would be very difficult to set out a concept of social justice that satisfies all these ends. Any particular set of priorities would simply breed the resentment and opposition of those who disagree with it. Hayek suggests that it is better for people to be left to pursue their own private ends. He says that this is best achieved through the free market.

None of Hayek's objections are fatal to the concept of positive freedom (Plant 1996; Commission on Taxation and Citizenship 2000). Viewing freedom only in terms of freedom from restraint leads to absurd implications. This concept suggests that freedom can be measured by adding up the external constraints that are placed on individuals: the fewer the constraints, the freer a society. The problem with this, however, is that the index leads us to conclude that certain societies that most observers would ordinarily see as less free than others are in fact more free. It is plausible to suggest that those countries which are less advanced economically than others have less need for rules that help regulate and govern economy and society. For instance, North Korea probably has less need for regulations than Canada. While many commentators would see Canada as a freer society than North Korea, this concept of freedom suggests the reverse. That Canada ought to be seen as a freer country must mean that freedom cannot be understood in terms of restrictions alone. Canada would be seen as freer because people have a greater opportunity to pursue their ends, which points to an inextricable link between freedom and ability. Second, if we consider where the value of freedom from constraint resides, it is reasonable to suppose that this is based on the ability of people to do what they want without outside interference. This implies that freedom and ability are not in fact as categorically different as Hayek suggests (Plant 1996; Commission on Taxation and Citizenship 2000).

Similarly, his criticisms of social justice fail to convince. Hayek's view that the adverse consequences of markets can never be foreseen seems questionable. It seems reasonable to suppose that instances of market failure can be foreseen, and so can be a matter of justice. It is difficult to see why adverse consequences cannot be foreseen given that market liberals are eager to extol the virtues of markets based on the positive benefits of markets that they can foresee (Plant 1996; Commission on Citizenship and Taxation 2000). Furthermore, although Hayek is right to point to the importance of conflicts of ends, there are grounds for saying that he exaggerates the tensions that arise when trying to fashion a concept of social justice. While disagreements will inevitably emerge, there are likely to be substantial areas in which people agree. Moreover part of the purpose of politics is to engender agreement over policy issues and priorities through public discussion and debates. The scope for agreement undermines the argument based on a conflict of ends. Even if Hayek is correct about the existence of conflicts, however, his prescription that policy-makers should steer clear of making decisions about ends is unlikely to halt tensions. Not everyone is likely to concur with his position, not least those who see social justice as an important commitment. Furthermore, the contention that ends should not be taken into account when fashioning policy is itself an argument about ends. While Hayek is keen to stress that he is above distributive conflicts, it is doubtful whether he can avoid being embroiled in political conflicts when he sets out the rules that ought to govern a society. Rules are not free-standing but are shaped by political discussion. The relevance of politics means that his solution does not in fact resolve the problems that he identifies.

Conclusion

This chapter has looked at the goals that public services ought to satisfy. I have suggested that contemplating the ends that public services ought to achieve raises questions of citizenship, and I have outlined a model of citizenship based on capability and responsibility. Capability means that public authorities distribute resources so that individuals are able to be or do a variety of things. Enhancing the range of things that a person is able to do requires substantial resources from government. The provision of resources imposes a reciprocal obligation that individuals use these resources in a responsible fashion. I have also considered how this model fares in light of the challenges posed to public services by user expectations, globalisation, rising costs and the New Right critique. I have suggested that one of the attractions of capability and responsibility relates to the way in which these adapt to those challenges. Capabilities help provide people with the capacities to play an active role within public services, and this involvement is a possible way of dealing with user expectations. The capability approach allows different people to develop different states of being or doing. This means that the capability approach is sensitive to a diversity of goods and circumstances, which is a key aspect of globalisation. Collective taxation provides a foundation for the capability approach, although an emphasis on responsibility can provide a rationale for the imposition of user fees to supplement public funds. Capability and responsibility is a species of social citizenship, and I have sought to show that social citizenship is robust to a New Right critique.

Capability and responsibility lays the basis for an active model of citizenship, both inside and outside public services. Activity within public services can be conducted in two main ways, through people exercising voice or exit. Up to now, it is an open question as to whether activity should be attempted through voice only, exit only or voice and exit. The next chapter picks up this question and advances a case for the use of voice and exit.

3 Problems of Central Planning

Introduction

In Chapter 2, I set out a model of citizenship based on the individual capacity to function as well as the exercise of individual responsibility. As part of this discussion, I suggested that there is a case for providing resources to individuals so that they will be able to play an active role within the public services they experience. This means that they are not simply passive recipients of public services. Instead, people have an active role to play in making decisions themselves. It was noted that this citizen participation could take one of two main forms. First, individuals could exercise voice, communicating their wishes to others and play a role in discussions about public services. Second, individuals can exercise choice. The particular type of choice highlighted was one where people express a choice between different providers.[1] Here, a person leaves one provider that they are unhappy with in favour of another. In Chapter 2, it was left an open question as to whether one or both of these routes ought to be used as a basis for participation. This chapter aims to provide an answer to this issue. It provides a case for utilising both voice and choice within public services.

My argument for voice and choice is based on a critical assessment of Friedrich Hayek's knowledge-based critique of central planning. As noted in Chapter 2, Hayek is the most important thinker of the New Right. As part of his engagement with the state, Hayek developed a knowledge-based critique of central planning. This knowledge-based argument forms the most important aspect of his thought (Hodgson 1999; Wainwright 2003). Hilary Wainwright writes that, 'Neo-liberalism owes its ability to reinvent itself ideologically to the foundations laid by Friedrich von Hayek. The central stone in these foundations was his critique of the "all-knowing state" in the name of practical, everyday knowledge' (Wainwright 2003, 16). Hayek's critique provides an argument for allowing choice within public services. The success of planning depends on the centre being able to devise and implement suitable plans. Knowledge and information is crucial for any set of plans to function well. If the centre is not to achieve a successful set of plans by accident, then it must know what is the best way of deploying resources at its disposal. Information has to be collected and processed and the appropriate levers of policy selected. Friedrich Hayek takes issue with the omniscient state. By undermining this assumption, Hayek seeks to demonstrate the failure of central planning. Hayek contends that the existence of practical or 'tacit' forms of knowledge means that the centre is unable to get access to the knowledge that is required for a comprehensive set of plans. Although Hayek provides a case for choice, there are limitations in his arguments. He over-looks the role that non-state collective forms of provision can play in the gen-eration of tacit knowledge. I suggest that tacit knowledge can take a variety of forms, and one version emerges from the interactions that people have with each other in a collective context. This provides a role for voice.

This chapter is organised as follows. First, I set out the background and main contours of Hayek's critique of central planning. I note the key to this critique rests on what he calls the division of knowledge problem. This means that the centre cannot get access to the knowledge that is dispersed throughout society. Tacit knowledge explains why this knowledge is inher-ently dispersed, and I note the connection he makes on competition as a way of co-ordinating such knowledge. In this section, I also comment on whether this knowledge is genuinely incapable of being expressed in a written form or whether it is simply knowledge left in a non-coded form. The second section moves on to consider a different model of tacit knowledge. This emphasises the generation of knowledge within a collective context, and I highlight how this approach can be detected in the resource-based or core-competence view of the firm. I note how stakeholding can help under-pin the creation of this knowledge and examine a challenge that casts doubt on whether voice is compatible with the generation of this tacit knowledge. The third section highlights how tacit knowledge provides a case for plural-ism in both the delivery and funding of public services. As part of this dis-cussion, I argue that the state has an important part to play in establishing the conditions under which such pluralism can occur. This role is bolstered by the presence of coded or explicit types of knowledge.

Background

Friedrich Hayek's critique of central planning has roots in a series of debates conducted during the 1920s and 1930s about whether a socialist economy based on a system of central planning could be just as efficient as markets. On the one side were those individuals who contended that central planning is a practical alternative to free markets. Not all of the individuals involved in this side of the dispute were committed socialists. Some, like Enrico Barone, were liberals, who nevertheless believed that as a matter of logic it could be demonstrated that a central planning regime could be just as efficient in allocating resources as a market-based system. Most of those involved in this side of the argument, however, were socialists. By showing that central planning was just as efficient in allocating resources as markets, they hoped to remove one of the key objections to socialism. To help support their case, theorists deployed one of the main methodological tools used to justify a commitment to markets. They wanted to illustrate that the same tools could be deployed to buttress the case for central planning. Theorists, in particular, drew upon the principles underpinning orthodox neoclassical economics. According to neoclassical economics, demand and supply within each market in an economy can be described by a set of equations. General equilibrium occurs when prices are set so that they solve all the equations at the same time. In other words, a set of prices can be found which clear all markets, so that demand equals supply in all markets. Enrico Barone (1908) argued that it was possible for a planner to arrive at the solution to the set of equations. Some theorists concede that it was sometimes not possible for a planner, at the first attempt, to find the set of prices that guarantee that all markets will clear. However, individuals such as Oskar Lange said that a market-based system could also be 'out of equilibrium'. A central planner could adopt the same procedure used in a market system. Advocates of markets argued that an 'auctioneer' could raise and lower prices through an auction so that all markets clear. Lange argued that a central planner could replicate this process to attain general equilibrium (Lange 1938).

On the other side of the argument were those people who rejected the idea that central planning could be as efficient in allocating resources as markets. This encompassed theorists such as Ludwig von Mises (1920) and F.A. Hayek. The nature of their contribution has been the subject of some debate. Don Lavoie (1985) notes that at the time it was widely thought that the arguments of these individuals rested on the view that the centre lacked the calculational capabilities to process the mass of knowledge in the economy. This argument over whether or not the centre could engage in such calculation led to these disputes being called the 'socialist calculation' debates. Lavoie argues that during the period the supporters of central planning were thought to have triumphed over their critics. It was thought that the centre could develop an algorithm capable of processing the mass of information that it received. Abram Bergson gives a snapshot of this general view when, in an article written during the 1940s summing up the debates, he said, 'there can hardly be any room for debate; of course socialism can work' (Bergson 1948, 447). The judgement that the criticisms of central planning had failed was questioned, however, by a later generation of theorists. Lavoie contends that the conclusion that Mises and Hayek failed is unsound because the nature of their arguments had not been properly understood. If the content of their arguments had in fact been correctly appreciated at the time, then the outcome of the disputes would have been very different. The issue for people such as Hayek was not about whether the centre possessed the capability of processing the knowledge which it was able to collect, but whether in fact it could gain access to this knowledge at all. Israel Kirzner agrees with this position, although he differs from Lavoie over when the telling objections to central planning emerged. Kirzner argues that although the germ of the 'Austrian school' critique was present during the calculation controversies, it had not been fully articulated during the 1930s. It was only developed later by Hayek (Kirzner 1988). Although Lavioe and Kirzner differ about when the Austrian critique was fully expressed, they concur that once articulated it convincingly undermined the case for central planning.

Hayek's critique of central planning

In the space below it is not possible to do justice to the full range and complexity of Hayek's thought. Nevertheless, it is possible to distil the principal elements of his approach. Hayek's theory of knowledge has several salient aspects. One of his core emphases concerns the dispersed or fragmented nature of knowledge (Gamble 1996).

Hayek writes that the knowledge,

> which we must make use never exists in a concentrated or integrated form but solely as the dispersed bits of incomplete and frequently contradictory knowledge which all the separate individuals possess. The economic problem of society is ... how to secure the best use of resources known to any of the members of society, for ends whose relative importance only those individuals know. Or to put it briefly, it is a problem of the utilization of knowledge which is not given to anyone in its totality (Hayek 1949, 77–78).

Hayek contends that knowledge is dispersed throughout the economy. He suggests that the imperative for policy is how best to cope with this dispersed knowledge. He argues, however, that in spite of the importance of this issue, it has not received the attention it deserves. He argues that the division of knowledge is at least as important an issue within economics as the division of labour. He contends, however, that while the latter has been the subject of much analysis, the former has been an unjustly neglected topic (Hayek 1949). The emphasis on the fragmented or dispersed nature of knowledge raises at least two issues. The first concerns why knowledge is thought to be dispersed. The second relates to why knowledge is seen as being *intrinsically* dispersed. An important part of Hayek's view about why knowledge is dispersed seems to be connected with his notion of the subjective character of knowledge. Hayek accepts that there exists a world that is outside and independent of each individual. People experience this world through their senses. Since knowledge is not simply a product of individual imagination and corresponds in some sense to an external reality, Hayek is pointing to an objective dimension to knowledge. He believes, however, that knowledge does not result from individuals simply receiving this 'sense-data'. People have a capacity independent of the external world to organise and interpret the data that they detect (Hayek 1976[1952]). The subjective aspect helps explain why knowledge is dispersed among the population. This is because knowledge is conditional in important part on subjective interpretation.

While the subjective character of knowledge helps understand why knowledge is dispersed across society, it does not on its own explain why this knowledge is intrinsically fragmented. Individuals might be able to write down the subjective knowledge they possess. They could then communicate this to the centre. A central planner, after gathering the mass of subjective knowledge that exists in an economy, may be able to process this in order to make appropriate decisions. If the knowledge is to be necessarily dispersed, the subjective knowledge must possess some other characteristic. Hayek alludes in his writings to its 'tacit' nature. This is Hayek's distinctive contribution to the socialist calculation debates. Stavros Ioannides comments that, 'what distinguishes Hayek's contribution in the debate is the notion of *tacit* knowledge' (Ioannides 2000, 46). Tacit knowledge refers to knowledge that is difficult to write down. Hayek suggests in his writings that an important part of the subjective knowledge that an individual possesses is of a tacit character. The sensory order is difficult to describe in important part because, we are not explicitly aware of the relations between the different qualities but merely manifest these relations in the discriminations which we perform, and because the number and complexity of these relations is probably greater than anything which we could ever explicitly state or exhaustively describe (Hayek 1976, 19).

Hayek says that his view is closely related to a distinction between 'knowing how' and 'knowing that' developed by Gilbert Ryle (Hayek 1976[1952]). Ryle drew attention to two kinds of knowledge. The first type he said consisted of the knowledge that individuals could explicitly articulate and write down. This knowledge is often expressed as a body of theoretical propositions. He called this 'knowledge that' and suggested that this was what people usually referred to when discussing knowledge. He said, however, that there exists a second type which he dubs 'knowledge how'. This concerns knowledge that is not possible to be explicitly stated. Much of this is rooted in practical experience and people acquire this through 'learning by doing'. Ryle argued that the role of knowing how had often been overlooked (Ryle 2000 [1949]). Hayek was drawn to knowing how in his theory of knowledge (Hayek 1967). Tacit knowledge creates a problem for a planner because it means the centre is denied access to a pool of knowledge it needs for efficiency. Thus, the centre faces a more radical difficulty than the need to process knowledge for effective public policy: it cannot even get access to this knowledge in the first place.

Competition and discovery

Friedrich Hayek's arguments highlight the shortcomings of relying on the centre to deliver public services. Hayek suggests that the best way to co-ordinate this dispersed knowledge is by relying on competition. Hayek argues that economic actors discover the best way of exploiting economic opportunities by experimenting with different strategies and ideas. Competition is important because it stimulates the trial of ideas. Although Hayek accepts that competition can be executed in a number of ways, he argues that competition is best conducted through the free market. Hayek believes that this conception helps us understand the true value of competition. He argues that in mainstream economics competition is seen as a mechanism for allocating resources. According to the orthodox position, the facts about resources are already known. He writes that, 'it starts from the assumption of a "given" supply of scarce goods. But which goods are scarce goods, or which things are goods, and how scarce or valuable they are – these are precisely the things that competition has to discover' (Hayek 1978, 181). Hayek argues that if the facts about goods were already known, it is difficult to see why competition is valuable. Rivalry between firms would be inefficient because when they duplicate efforts to produce a commodity they engage in a wasteful use of scarce resources. Hayek argues that the true role of competition turns the orthodox logic on its head. Competition acts as a way of discovering the very facts about scarcity of goods that the orthodox stance assumes is already known.

Tacit or non-coded knowledge?

Friedrich Hayek highlights the role that tacit knowledge plays in limiting the capacity of the centre to undertake effective central planning. One issue raised by this critique is whether or not the knowledge to which Hayek alludes is truly incapable of being expressed in a coded form. This objection is important because it is likely to mean that Hayek's critique is less far-reaching than it currently stands (though this is not to say that it would be insignificant). For example, Cowan et al. (2000) accept that there exists a body of knowledge within the economy that is not formally expressed. They deny, however, that such knowledge is not coded because it is incapable of being written down. They say that it is feasible to express all knowledge in a coded form. Such 'translation' involves the use of a 'codebook'. The codebook is like a dictionary, which provides a way of expressing knowledge in a coded form. They say that codifying a piece of knowledge draws on existing contents of a codebook and also (once codified) adds content to the codebook. Robin Cowan, Paul David and Dominique Foray argue that the only reason why knowledge is left in a non-coded form is because the benefits of codifying knowledge are outweighed by its costs. This situation may change if technologies are developed that reduce the costs of codifying knowledge. They say that this underlines the fact that the boundary between coded and tacit knowledge is not fixed. It shifts as technology changes. Cowan and colleagues contend that emphasis should be placed on expanding the body of coded knowledge. This implies focusing attention on reducing the costs of codifying knowledge.

Empirical studies are likely to be important for deciding whether or not knowledge can be really tacit. I suggest that evidence exists which supports the idea of a tacit dimension to knowledge. For example, Harry Collins has sought to provide empirical evidence through his case studies on scientific practice. In particular, he claims that scientists often find it difficult to replicate the experimental results of others simply by following their written procedures. Such problems can often be overcome when the scientist or teams of scientists who are trying to repeat the results observe those who successfully carried out the experiment. Collins suggests that a central reason for this is that a significant part of the knowledge involved in conducting such experiment is tacit which cannot be transferred through formal instruction. His examination of the 'Q' factor of sapphire is a recent example of his case studies. Collins notes that a team of researchers at Moscow State University have claimed, since the late 1970s, to be able to detect a high Q value associated with sapphire. The Q factor is a measure indicating how pure a substance is (the higher the Q, the purer the material). Collins states that efforts to replicate these findings elsewhere in Europe and the United States had not borne fruit throughout the 1980s and most of the 1990s. He argues that in the summer of 1999 one of the members of the Russian team (whom he dubs 'Checkhov') visited a team of researchers based at the University of Glasgow. The Glasgow academics observed the Russian scientist conducting experiments on sapphire. Subsequently, the scientists in Scotland were able to repeat the high Q value found for sapphire. Collins suggests that the reason why scientists based outside Moscow were unable to mirror their findings was in large part because they lacked the tacit knowledge possessed by the Russians. This knowledge became more readily available to individuals in Glasgow after they had seen Checkhov at work. Jan Magnus and Mary Morgan (1999) tested for tacit knowledge within the domain of econometrics. Econometrics tries to find the quantitative relationship that best explains one particular variable in terms of a series of other variables. For instance, it aims to show how incidence of unemployment is influenced by age, gender and education. Magnus and Morgan asked a student who was relatively inexperienced in econometrics to try to replicate an analysis on a particular dataset by an expert. The student only had access to written methodologies of acknowledged 'masters' as well as examples of applied analysis. The student wrote down the steps they followed in an accompanying logbook. Various experts were then asked to comment on the student's work. Magnus and Morgan found that the student encountered difficulties in replicating the results of the masters' analysis. Magnus and Morgan say that the reason for this is that an important element of econometric procedures involved choices and judgement calls. They argue that these judgements cannot be reduced to formal rules, but are instead grounded in tacit knowledge.

Even if one is not persuaded by the above empirical studies, and believe that all knowledge is capable of being expressed in an explicit format, there are reasons for preferring to develop institutions that deal with non-coded knowledge rather than putting efforts simply on coding all knowledge. As Robin Cowan, Paul David and Dominique Foray accept, the costs of coding knowledge may often outweigh the benefits of doing so. Moreover, even if technology develops so that the costs of turning non-coded into coded forms are less, it ought to be borne in mind that the benefits of coding this knowledge is likely to yield diminishing returns. Dan Corry and Gerry Stoker (2002) point out that the larger the volume of data that the centre has to process, the more decision-making is likely to be clogged up. Coding knowledge probably yields diminishing returns, and even if the cost of turning knowledge into coded knowledge falls, a concomitant fall in benefits is likely to mean that in an important set of cases, the costs of coding still outweigh the benefits. Moreover, Johnson et al. (2002) argue that emphasis placed on codification tends to assume that coded knowledge is superior to non-coded forms and that this assumption is questionable. I shall proceed by assuming that it is reasonable to suppose the existence of tacit or practical forms of knowledge. However, even if one rejects this particular assumption, the existence of a significant pool of non-coded knowledge means that the analysis below should still be of relevance.

Collective models of tacit knowledge

We have seen that Hayek provides a case for the use of competition to discover knowledge. While I believe that there is merit in this suggestion, I do not think that an analysis of knowledge ought to be confined to its discovery. Knowledge is also plausibly generated or created as well as discovered. In fact, this assumption is one of the main ways that various observers on the left who are sympathetic to Hayek's critique of central planning have nevertheless sought to respond to his arguments. Hilary Wainwright says

> recognition of both the importance of practical knowledge (as against the assumptions of traditional social engineering) and the social, sharable nature of knowledge (as against the assumptions of neo-liberalism) provides a vital foundation stone for a genuine 'third way' (Wainwright 2003, 26).

Wainwright accepts Hayek's critique of the centralised state, but challenges his view that tacit knowledge is best seen in terms of individuals acting on their own. Wainwright points to the social character of tacit knowledge, and the rationale this provides for collective institutions that exist beneath the level of the state. This alternative approach rests on the assumption that teamwork can help generate organisational 'know-how'. A team is a collection of individuals that work together to achieve some common goal or goals. When people work together, they can develop patterns of interactions or routines. These routines can endow a firm with value as they help capture productive ways that individuals can work alongside each other. These practices may develop through a process of trial-and-error and are hard to capture through formal codes. Instead, a sense of know-how develops between different people that constitute a source of organisational knowledge.

Organisational know-how points to the creation of tacit knowledge within a collective context. Collective arenas can take a variety of forms, ranging from the state to local bodies. The state is not an appropriate forum, however, for the generation of this tacit knowledge because of the difficulties in fashioning regular and face-to-face relationships. Teams depend on their members being in fairly regular contact with one another. As the members of the team increase, it becomes more difficult to guarantee regular relationships. Diaries have to be reconciled, and this task is made harder as the number of diaries to be co-ordinated increases. The population of a state is likely to be too large to be able to sustain such regular participation. In addition, practical knowledge requires some degree of face-to-face interaction. This contact acts as a way of transmitting knowledge that cannot be easily written down. The large area typically spanned by the state is probably not conducive to such interactions. The collective arenas that are most suitable for the formation of this tacit knowledge are local bodies that operate below the level of the state.

The teamwork framework recognises the contribution that different individuals in different parts of the organisation can make towards the creation of tacit knowledge. In doing this, this approach is drawn to acknowledging the role of different stakeholders. Various conditions need to be in place, however, if the different stakeholders are to work together. They must have channels through which they can interact and exchange ideas. This intersects with the sorts of institutions associated with stakeholding, such as participation on company boards. There is a connection between collective forms of tacit knowledge and stakeholding. This can be seen if we examine the programmes of those putting forward collective models of tacit knowledge. For example, Geoff Hodgson (1999) argues for an economy based on the generation of organisational know-how. He suggests that organisational structures help to provide a foundation for this knowledge and that these structures are likely to embrace an important role for stakeholding. The notion of organisational know-how is not entirely new, and has important roots within the core-competence or resource-based theories of the firm. Indeed, contemporary advocates of tacit knowledge often draw on this literature when developing their own proposals (Hodgson 1999; Leadbeater 2000). Edith Penrose is one of the key contributors to this business literature. In *The Theory of the Growth of the Firm*, Penrose sought to analyse the growth of the modern firm. She believed that growth originates from a variety of sources. She says that one important source of the growth of firms is achieved through the growth in capabilities. Here the firm develops competencies to perform certain tasks. It could, for example, acquire capabilities to provide an ever-wider range of goods or services. These competencies provide a set of resources the managers of a firm could draw upon as they compete in the marketplace. For Penrose resources include tangible things such as plant, equipment and land as well as human resources such as skilled and unskilled labour. One of the key resources Penrose drew attention to was the knowledge generated when people within the firm acted as a team. She points to two types of knowledge that emerges within this context. The first 'objective' kind, 'can be formally taught, can be learned from other people or from the written word, and can, if necessary, be formally expressed and transmitted to others' (Penrose 1959, 53). When people participate in a team they develop patterns of working together or routines. Penrose suggests that part of these routines can be formally expressed. Members can codify some of the best ways that people can co-operate with each other (for example what procedures to adopt during production) and communicate this to others. If a person leaves a team, then that part of their role that can be written down can be transmitted straightforwardly to a newcomer. By following the instructions they are given, the newcomer can replicate this part of the activities of their predecessor fairly easily. The second kind was rooted in practical experience and could not be easily replaced if personnel left a firm. She says that experience

produces increased knowledge about things and contributes to 'objective' knowledge in so far as its results can be transmitted to others. But experience itself can never be transmitted; it produces a change – frequently a subtle change – in individuals and cannot be separated from them (Penrose 1959, 53).

Penrose here is alluding to the sort of organisational knowledge that has been discussed above. She makes the point that this knowledge takes time to develop, and cannot be easily transmitted to a newcomer after a person has left the organisation.

Criticisms of collective models

Collective models of tacit knowledge have not gone unchallenged. Supporters of Hayek have claimed that his critique of central planning in fact extends to all collective forms of intervention. For these commentators, local bodies as well as the state are vulnerable to his criticisms. Mark Pennington (2003) argues that a common theme in collective forms of tacit knowledge is a connection that is made between 'deliberative democracy' and practical knowledge. Deliberative democracy is a model of democracy that emphasises the role of discussion between different individuals. Rather than conceiving democracy as a mechanism for simply aggregating or adding up individual preferences, deliberative democracy stresses the role of discussion as a way of shaping these preferences. Individuals come together to deliberate common problems, and in this process they may change their opinions and ideally arrive at common solutions. Deliberation requires arenas where people can realistically come together, and these will tend to be in small-scale collective contexts of the sort described immediately above. The exercise of voice is thus key to deliberative democracy. Mark Pennington argues that deliberation can only transmit knowledge capable of being expressed in a verbal form. He adds that tacit knowledge cannot be articulated and so deliberation is not well suited to the transmission of tacit knowledge. Pennington concludes that the attempt to ground tacit knowledge in deliberative democracy is flawed and so rejects collective models of tacit knowledge. He contends that, 'Hayekian arguments against orthodox socialist planning models may also be turned against the normative claims made by deliberative democrats' (Pennington 2003, 726).

Mark Pennington's critique of deliberative democracy extends to my discussion of stakeholding. This is because stakeholding is intended to underpin the sort of dialogue or voice associated with deliberative democracy. Although Pennington is right that tacit knowledge cannot be expressed in a verbal format, his own arguments can be used to show how voice may have a useful role to play in relation to tacit knowledge. Pennington argues that although tacit knowledge cannot itself be expressed in a verbal form, it can nevertheless be transferred between people through non-verbal channels. In particular, an individual can get access to the tacit knowledge of an experienced partner by observing and imitating their actions. He writes that tacit knowledge, 'can only be revealed through social action, such as exchange or the exercise of a skill, and passed on to others via a process of imitation' (Pennington 2003, 731).

Although imitation may be an important part of non-verbal communication, this does not mean that imitation only occurs through non-vocal channels. An agent may be able to communicate formally some basic instructions or skills that help define a framework for imitation, and these instructions may give rise to tacit knowledge. Mari Sako provides an example of this in her analysis of industrial clusters within Japan. Sako takes as her starting point the importance of the 'core-competence' view of firms mentioned above. She argues that an important part of knowledge-based resources are tacit in character. She contends that clusters often arise as a way of trying to foster the transfer of a firm's distinctive but hard to imitate knowledge-based resources. Using a study of the relationship that the Toyota motor company in Japan has with their suppliers to illustrate her case, she says that employees of the suppliers often give an insight into their working practices to Toyota. By observing these working practices, managers at Toyota help improve the way the different parts are assembled. It benefits the car manufacturer by helping avoid various difficulties in the production process, and this helps suppliers because Toyota finds it valuable to maintain links with suppliers because they have access to their 'know-how'. Sako says that as part of this process, Toyota employees deliver lectures on their working methods. Thus, although Sako accepts the significance of tacit knowledge, her analysis shows the ways that voice can be used to support knowledge transfer (Sako 1999). I suggest that while it is true that voice and tacit knowledge are different, there are grounds for suggesting they are not incompatible.

Ikujiro Nonaka and Hirotaka Takeuchi (1995) consider a model in which tacit and explicit knowledge, though distinct, are in a mutually supportive relationship. Nonaka and Takeuchi outline four different modes of conversion between the different types of knowledge. First, tacit knowledge can be 'converted' into tacit knowledge. In this situation the tacit knowledge possessed by one individual is 'acquired' by another person. They suggest that the apprenticeship system is a central way that this occurs. In particular, a master craftsman or craftswoman gains tacit knowledge through practical experience. An apprentice gains access to some of this tacit knowledge by observing and imitating a master. Nonaka and Takeuchi call this a process of 'socialization'. Second, they note a conversion process from tacit to explicit knowledge (which they dub 'externalization'). The way this occurs for these authors is complex and involves a series of steps. Individuals meet and by using metaphors and analogies try to communicate some of the tacit knowledge that they possess. The core ideas and assumptions that inform these metaphors are then set out and distilled. This provides the basis for an explicit body of knowledge that 'converts' the tacit into explicit knowledge. Turning explicit knowledge into explicit knowledge is the third feature they highlight. In this scenario, elements of an existing body of knowledge are often combined with other forms of explicit knowledge (and so is called 'combination'). They say that combination often occurs within information processing. Finally, they point to a move from explicit to tacit knowledge. Denoting this 'internalization', they say that individuals absorb or internalize explicit knowledge. This then animates their practical activity, which then acts as a source of tacit knowledge gained through learning by doing. All of these different aspects interact to foster a 'knowledge creating spiral'. Tacit knowledge originally communicated through a process of socialization is eventually 'externalized' into an explicit form. This allows it to be combined with other forms of explicit knowledge. The results of this combination are then 'internalized'.

Pluralism in delivery

I have pointed above to two different conceptions of tacit knowledge. A Hayekian strand highlights the importance of tacit knowledge that people acquire through practical activity on their own and stresses the role that competition plays in co-ordinating this dispersed knowledge. Collectivist models emphasise the generation of tacit knowledge between different individuals and spotlights the part played by co-operation. One approach to public policy is to stress the role of one or other of these models of tacit knowledge. This is often the position of the analysts mentioned above. For example, Mark Pennington (2003) accepts Hayek's conception of tacit knowledge but rejects the version associated with deliberative democrats. My own view is that both camps contain important insights and that these models are not mutually exclusive. I think that some knowledge is dispersed throughout the economy and society and that competition can act as a discovery mechanism. However, I also believe that it is possible for people to create knowledge by working together, and part of this cannot be easily written down. This means that there is a role for competition and co-operation or, more broadly, choice and voice. Of course, one might reject my judgement and choose instead to emphasise either the creation or discovery of tacit knowledge but not both. Furthermore, even if one accepts a role for both creation and discovery, one might argue that the relationship between these two types of knowledge is the result of conscious institutional choices (and so one can shape tacit knowledge in a number of directions). This means that underlining the importance of both discovery and creation leaves open the large question of how the balance between these two types of knowledge ought to be struck. Whatever one's conception of tacit knowledge, I suggest that this type of knowledge provides an impulse for a pluralism of providers within public services. Although the precise nature of policy is likely to vary depending on the specific stance one adopts towards tacit knowledge. I contend that all standpoints provide a case for a range of different organisations within public services.

Both the Hayekian and collectivist models agree on the difficulty of accommodating this type of knowledge (either co-ordination or generation) within the structures of the state. Hayek's emphasis on competition implies the existence of a range of providers. In terms of the character of these providers, a connection is often made within the New Right between competition and the profit motive. In particular, what provides individuals or organisations with an incentive to compete is the prospect of being able to capture material rewards (Hayes 1994). This line of thought suggests that if we try to inject competition within public services, then we must allow providers to make profits. I think that although the role of profits ought to be acknowledged, competition does not have to rely on the profit motive alone. I do not think that agents are only drawn to compete by the prospect of material gains. Individuals or organisations might be motivated to compete by a desire to deliver a good service to users. We have seen that a service ethic plays an important role in the motivations of public servants, and that there is a preference to work for 'mission-oriented' organisations. It is possible that such mission-oriented organisations can compete with each other. Although one might argue that the profit motive is the most important motive for competition, I do not think that one can rule out the existence of other motivations. This means that 'non-profit' bodies might have a useful role alongside for-profit provision. I contend that Hayek's knowledge-based arguments provide an additional rationale for a plurality of provision that contains a role for non-profit alongside for-profit providers. Hayek's belief in the dispersed or fragmented nature of knowledge presumably extends to organisational types. No one knows what organisational forms are best suited to all sectors of an economy at any given time. This provides a case for pluralism in organisational forms delivering public services. This pluralism applies to the objectives that these organisations follow. Consequently, Hayek's arguments allow a role for non-profit and for-profit bodies. Collectivist models concentrate on the creation of knowledge within a local environment. Differences are likely to occur between different organisations for a host of reasons. Different stakeholders will be important in different areas of the public services. Within transport, stakeholders will probably include employees, passengers and engineering firms. Within education, stakeholders include parents, teachers and pupils. Even if we confine our attention to a particular sector, differences are likely to emerge in different parts of the country. Within health, for example, not all hospitals will have access to a university medical or dental school. Those areas that do have such schools will have a different set of stakeholders. Different institutional policies may also be needed to involve a particular set of stakeholders in different parts of the country. For example, patients from minority ethnic communities may face particular barriers to access hospitals in specific parts of the country, and overcoming these barriers may require measures to be enacted. Allowing organisations to develop their own unique set of practices or routines is also a source of difference, and therefore pluralism, within public services. In terms of objectives, models of organisational knowledge are neutral between the pursuit of profit and non-profit goals. Collectivist models of tacit knowledge can be conjoined with a commitment to the public interest, and this may be appropriate in situations where both users and public servants place emphasis on the importance of a service ethic and the public interest. It is possible, however, to achieve organisational knowledge with profits. We have noted that resource-based theories of the firm provide one of the roots of organisational knowledge. Within this literature, this type of knowledge is often presented as a strategy that a firm can adopt to enhance profits (Kay 1996). While many users and public servants may wish to work for bodies dedicated to the public interest, others might be happy to be involved with those bodies that pursue profit. This means that collectivist knowledge supports a pluralism of provision that allows a role for both non-profit and for-profit provision.

The role of the state

I have argued above that the different approaches to tacit knowledge provide a case for pluralism within the system of delivery. This emphasis on pluralism does not rule out, however, a role for the state. In relation to tacit knowledge, the state has a part to play in providing the conditions under which alternative organisational forms can flourish. Some commentators suggest that decisions about organisational forms are best left to the market. If a specific organisation is suitable in a particular context, then managers of the organisation will be driven to adopt this form on their own account. Thus, if stakeholding enhances corporate performance, then executives will be motivated to implement stakeholder policies on their own accord without intervention by the state (Willetts 1997). In response to this argument, I return to my point that markets are not free-standing entities but are instead constituted and regulated by social rules and norms. The state can play a valuable role in creating this framework of rules, and so can be involved in laying the ground for the subsequent emergence of different organisational forms. For example, the way that companies are constituted depends in part on the provisions of the law. Company law may only recognise the legitimacy of one particular type, and this forecloses the development of other organisational structures. For instance, company law may prioritise a limited company or plc form. This is a shareholder model of the firm that limits the liability of shareholders up to a specified amount in the event that the firm goes bankrupt. Company law might alternatively set out rules that allow the creation of a range of organisational forms, such as the public interest company.

My focus above has been on knowledge that is embodied in practical experience and which cannot be written down. Although this discussion highlights the significance of tacit knowledge, not all knowledge is of a tacit variety. Some knowledge can be written down or expressed in a coded format. Traditionally, studies of knowledge refer to knowledge of this kind. The role of coded knowledge is recognised by most of the analysts of tacit knowledge discussed above. Edith Penrose alludes to coded knowledge in her discussion of objective knowledge, Ikujiro Nonaka and Hirotaka Takeuchi refer to explicit knowledge and Gilbert Ryle points to the part played by 'knowing that'. Indeed, we have seen that for some commentators all forms of knowledge can in fact be expressed in a formal or coded format.

State intervention is also bolstered by the existence of coded knowledge. I suggest that coded knowledge allows a useful role to be played by central institutions. Part of this is intended to help guarantee that users of services enjoy a minimum level of service, whichever part of the country they inhabit. The existence of coded knowledge creates the possibility that the centre may be able to formulate and regulate centrally defined standards. In addition, coded knowledge may mean that there are situations in which the centre can collect and co-ordinate some of the knowledge needed for an effective system of planning and intervention. Some evidence of the positive role that the centre can undertake can be seen by considering the benefits of the literacy hour within primary schools in England. Stephen Machin and Sandra McNally (2003) note that the literacy hour was introduced into around 400 English primary schools between 1997 and 1998. The central government provides guidelines on strategies to promote literacy, and children in these schools were exposed to this policy for about two years before a National Literacy Strategy was rolled out nationally. In an evaluation of this policy, Machin and McNally argue that substantial improvements in reading and English have occurred. Moreover, this initiative is not very expensive, which means that this is good value for money.

Although coded knowledge can provide the basis for an effective system of central planning, I do not believe that forming such plans is an easy matter or is without problems. One issue relates to the volume of knowledge that the centre has to handle. We have seen above that the socialist calculational disputes focused on whether or not the centre could process the knowledge at its disposal. At the time it did seem that the centre could process this knowledge. Today, developments in computer technology seem to have bolstered this judgement. Although computers have arguably made the mechanics of calculation easier, technology can act as a double-edged sword. The ease with which coded knowledge can now be communicated to the centre has also been made easier, with the result that the centre can face a larger volume of data to process than in the past. Dan Corry and Gerry Stoker suggest that the centre will be overwhelmed by the flood of information that it receives and this will stymie decision-making. They contend that the, 'total flow of paper or e-mails is always more then they can digest. As a result, people at the centre are always time challenged, and only able to focus on a limited number of issues' (Corry and Stoker 2002, 15). It is possible that the problems of co-ordination are of a much higher order than in the past, notwithstanding the progress of computer technology. In contemporary circumstances, judgements about the viability of calculation may need to be overturned. Even if one believes that calculation is still feasible, it is important to register that local organisations may not have an incentive to transfer knowledge to the centre. Local bodies who perform well under a centralised system are likely both to exaggerate their own achievements and resist passing on lessons to others for fear of losing their privileged position with the centre. Thus, even though knowledge is in principle capable of being communicated to the centre, and a central planner is capable of devising plans, local institutions might not want to transfer this knowledge. Although coded knowledge helps provide a case for central planning, I do not think it provides it with unqualified support. Constraints exist over the efficiency of central planning, even in the case of coded knowledge.

Funding

I have suggested that the existence of tacit knowledge provides a case for pluralism within the delivery of public services. Although the existence of tacit knowledge means that the centre will still have an important role within provision, the presence of practical knowledge provides an argument for going beyond the state. I also wish to suggest that knowledge-based arguments carry implications for the funding of public services. This is in terms of the character of public funding as well as the role that may be allowed for private finance.

In the opening chapter, I argued that the existence of market failure means that an adequate system of public funding must depend importantly on the public purse. Taxation is crucial for these public funds, either through taxes that raise money immediately or through deferred taxation which is used to pay for public borrowing. Although the public purse is key to the funding of public services, public monies can be spent in a variety of ways. The centre could make spending decisions, planning the budgets of police forces, rail networks and water suppliers. A different approach is for the centre to raise money but allow local bodies or individuals considerable autonomy over how this money is spent. Another issue concerns who should receive public money. One model of funding pays money to the providers of these services. Historically, this has been the dominant mode of funding within a state-centred model of public services. Here money goes directly to schools or hospitals. An alternative model is for the money to go to the user rather than the provider. This could be done through a publicly funded voucher scheme. Parents could be provided with vouchers which they could use to purchase primary education for their children. Alternatively, people who have to rely on 'home helps' may be provided with direct payments from their local authority which they would use to purchase care services for their homes.

I suggest that the critique of central planning set out in this chapter extends to a model of public finance driven by the centre. The centre encounters the same sort of barriers to knowledge that it confronts in relation to the provision of public services. This provides a case for allowing local agents to have autonomy over how money is spent. This is not to say that the centre can have no role at all within spending. I have suggested that it is useful to combine a focus on central standards with local autonomy. This helps ensure that all providers will attempt to deliver a minimum level of service. Furthermore, the presence of coded knowledge means that the centre may be capable of setting out some efficient and effective plans. Although the centre can play a useful role in spending, tacit knowledge provides backing for local autonomy.

The different models of tacit knowledge have an impact on the form that public spending should take. Applying Hayek's arguments in relation to funding provides some support for the use of voucher schemes. Providing users with vouchers helps people to exercise choice and sustain a degree of competition. Tom Miers (2003) deploys this perspective in his advocacy of vouchers in education or health. Miers argues that choice and competition are essential for high quality public services. He contends that competition and choice provides incentives for suppliers to improve quality and cost, and act as a way of co-ordinating information throughout an economy. He contrasts this with a state-centred approach which he says lacks the incentives to improve service and affordability as well as the capacity to undertake efficient co-ordination. Miers says that vouchers are a way of promoting choice. He contends that typically voucher schemes allow individuals to trade a voucher with a fixed amount for a given level of service. Miers contends that while such schemes will help deliver improvements in service quality, they do not harness the potential for competition on price. To allow the benefits of competition on price and quality, Miers advocates a set of Public Service Allowances (PSAs). These are accounts which contain funds dedicated for the purchase of health and education. Individuals would be provided with funds equalling the average cost of paying for health or education. Rather than trading a voucher worth a fixed amount, individuals have flexibility over how their budget is allocated. Miers proposes that providers would be allowed to charge different amounts for services. He argues that PSAs will help engender competition in terms of price as well as quality, and suggests that this will reap the full benefits of competition.

While I recognise a role for vouchers, I do not think that public funds should not be distributed through vouchers alone. Public service providers usually require substantial resources in order to be established. Schools need buildings and staff, and hospitals require medical equipment. In the private sector, these start-up and maintenance costs are usually raised through the issue of equity or shares, or through borrowing from capital markets. Market failure means that public services cannot rely principally on these sources of funds. In this situation, there is a case for government to provide at least some money direct to public service providers. These will help these organisations undertake necessary investment. The emphasis on stakeholding also provides reasons for giving some money to providers. Voucher schemes put purchasing power in the hands on one particular type of stakeholder, the user. This is intended to help services be driven by user concerns. If we view the purpose of services to foster a web of relationships among different stakeholders, then I believe there is an argument for providing money to managers to help establish and maintain their relationships with providers. I suggest that public funds might be usefully divided into payments to the provider and the user, although the precise balance between this is likely to vary over time and between different parts of the public services.

In addition to the points made about public funds, I believe that knowledge-based arguments support the use of private finance within public services. Innovation is likely to be an important feature of services. Innovation will help providers adapt to the changing and rising expectations of their users, as well as delivering improvements in the quality of service provided to users. A belief in the dispersed and fragmented nature of knowledge implies that no agency – either public or private – has privileged access to what investment projects will succeed. No one possesses an intrinsic capacity to 'pick winners'. I suggest that applying the idea of competition to innovation means that one should allow both public and private bodies to fund innovation. Competition between these agencies will help fuel discovery.

Conclusion

In this chapter I have examined Friedrich Hayek's knowledge-based critique of central planning. Hitherto, I do not think this critique has received the attention it deserves. I am not saying that Hayek's arguments have been entirely ignored (we have seen that Hilary Wainwright and Geoff Hodgson refer to his work), but that they are worthy of further exploration. Hayek is important because he develops what is arguably the most powerful critique from the New Right of a programme of central planning. I suggest that the issue of tacit or practical knowledge poses a core problem for the effectiveness of a system guided by the centre. While Hayek is right to warn against central planning, he overlooks the ways that tacit knowledge may be generated in a collective context. This means that rather than simply emphasising the market and competition as he suggests, there is a space for collective institutions that operate beneath the level of the state. Practical knowledge lends itself to pluralism in the delivery and funding of public services. In addition, the presence of coded knowledge means that the centre can still play an important role, albeit one that is much more limited than an approach driven by the centre.

4 Organisational Issues

In the previous two chapters I have presented an argument for a 'pluralistic' model of public services that allows users a role for both choice and voice within public services. To recap, in Chapter 2, I suggested that despite the criticisms of the New Right, the notion of social citizenship is still a worthy aim of public policy. Social citizenship should be able to adapt, however, to the complexity that characterises much of modern society, and I proposed that the capability approach could play a valuable role in this regard. The capability approach concentrates on people's capacity to function, and I suggested that that policy could focus on the capacity to function both inside and outside of public services. I continued that taking steps to increase the capacity to function within public services can help increase the responsiveness of services to users, which may help address the dissatisfaction that a substantial portion of users feel with their public services. Chapter 3 picked up this discussion by suggesting that both the main routes for participation, that is choice and voice, are likely to be important for encouraging user activity within public services. I examined Friedrich Hayek's knowledge-based critique of central planning and from this highlighted a valuable role for choice and voice for discovering and creating knowledge. The present chapter follows through what choice and voice may mean for the organisation of public services. What needs to be in place if we are to implement a system of choice and voice within public services? Put briefly, I suggest the importance of having a plural system of provision – which includes a role for the public and private sectors – within a framework of central standards.

Choice

This section of the chapter considers some of the important organisational features that should be in place to encourage a well-developed system of choice. I highlight three main features.

First, choice should be subject to a system of national and international regulation. Regulation is needed to deal with issues related to both users and providers. One concern with user choice relates to the possibility of social segregation. The idea is that when users are exercising choice among providers, one of the things that will influence their decision is the character of the other people who are being served by the provider. Users might select providers where most of the existing users match up to aspects of their own character, for example their racial, religious or class background. This means that choice may help fuel social segregation, with enclaves forming between people with different racial, religious or class characteristics. This creates a problem if this social segregation helps undermine the cohesiveness of society. In particular, lack of contact between people from different backgrounds might help foster ignorance about each other and allow myths to breed. These sources of misunderstanding could lead to conflicts of various sorts, which would undermine the cohesiveness of a society. User choice may weaken social cohesion (Perri 6 2003; Working Commission on Choice in K-12 Education 2004).

At least two qualifications can be added to the idea that user choice will weaken social cohesion. First, user choice may in some instances help improve social cohesion. In a society in which inability of a religious minority to be able to choose a particular religion-based education for their children is a source of disquiet and unhappiness for that minority, permitting parents to make some choices about the religious basis for their children's education may help integrate that minority more fully into the wider society and reduce tensions between the minority and majority communities. Second, problems of social cohesion exist in the absence of user choice. In a school system without direct parental choice, parents may be required to send their children to the nearest school. This neighbourhood-based schooling might still lead to segregation between schools as people from different class or racial backgrounds congregate in different neighbourhoods. Moreover, even if segregation does not occur between schools, and so different providers serve different types of people, segregation can still occur within schools as different groups form clusters within schools.

The absence of user choice does not mean, therefore, that problems of social cohesion will disappear. However, it might be the case that providing choice to the public may worsen social segregation, and this puts additional strain on social cohesion. In itself, this does not mean that user choice should be rejected. User choice will have a range of consequences for a variety of different values, and one ought to weigh-up or trade-off any increases in the responsiveness of services to individuals that choice helps engender with any losses in social cohesion that it brings about. Beyond this, various steps could be attempted to mitigate the effects of any social segregation. The Working Commission on Choice in K-12 Education (2004) in the

United States highlights several policies which could be developed to try to protect social cohesion. Schools could be required to teach civics courses as part of their curriculum. Pupils would be taught the values of equality, tolerance and democracy as part of these courses. The Commission says that incentives could be implemented to encourage effective teaching of civics courses. Positive student attitudes and good results in school exit examinations on such issues could attract rewards. The Commission adds that complaints procedures should be put in place to help ensure that schools do not engage in separatist teaching. These recommendations suggest a role for a system of national regulation of school activity, in helping outline the content of civics courses and in monitoring that schools abide by these commitments.

Regulations are also needed to protect the standards of service experienced by users. In the previous chapter, I argued for a plural system of funding and provision, where a range of providers – both public and private – can participate in the supply and financing of public services. It is likely that diverse outcomes will result from this diverse model of public services. I shall postpone a discussion of the link between pluralism and equality to a later chapter. For now, I wish to note that it is important to have a set of regulations to protect the standards experienced by users. David Miller (2005) argues that it is important when thinking about social justice to distinguish between principles of justice and the 'social minimum' required to achieve those principles of justice. He says that while citizenship helps define the principles of justice, the social minimum refers to the minimum amount of resources – such as health services – that are sufficient to achieve and maintain these principles of justice. The notion of a social minimum underlines the importance of public services delivering a minimum level of service (Marshall 1992; White 2003; Miller 2005). A system of regulation will be important for helping guarantee that services deliver this social minimum. It is likely that much of this will be pitched at a national level. Although national authorities will be important for helping monitor and police these national standards, the standards themselves need not be devised simply by national bodies. Users can participate in a variety of ways in helping set these standards, ranging from providing data which will help central bodies set standards to allowing users to vote on different service standards.

While securing the social minimum implies a focus on national system of regulation, there is also likely to be a role for international regulation. One of the facets of economic globalisation relates to the activities of multinational companies (Scholte 2000; Pierson 2001). Multinationals raise a

variety of issues for public services. One issue relates to the spread of
'transborder health risks'. Jeff Collin and Kelley Lee (2003) point out that
the reduction in barriers to trade, particularly in the Asia Pacific region, has
fuelled a growth in the tobacco industry. Between 1975 and 1996, the
consumption of cigarettes across the world rose by 50 per cent (Chaloupka
and Corbett 1998). A total of 5.3 trillion cigarettes were smoked in 1997
(Knight et al. 1998). Much of this expansion is driven by a handful of multinational companies. Three quarters of the world cigarette market is controlled by the following four companies: Philip Morris, British American
Tobacco, Japan Tobacco/R.J. Reynolds and the China National Tobacco
Corporation (Crescenti 1999). Between 1989 and 1998, Philip Morris saw
its international profits increase over fivefold to five billion dollars
(Joossens and Ritthiphakde 2000). This expansion of the global consumption of tobacco raises global issues because of the adverse impact that
smoking has on good health. Collin and Lee note that today around one in
ten adult deaths per year can be attributed to tobacco, and the total number
of deaths is expected to rise from four million to ten million deaths by 2030.
Seventy per cent of such deaths are expected to occur in the developing
world.

The activities of multinationals will depend on the role that they are
allowed by global community. Decisions made about whether or not companies are allowed to advertise their product on billboards or television,
whether or not tobacco firms can sponsor sporting events and whether or not
areas such as the Chinese market (which has hitherto not been subject to
international competition) should be opened up will all impact on the nature
of the tobacco market. In deciding the appropriate controls that ought to be
placed on the tobacco trade in view of the implications of such trade for ill
health, different countries will need forums at which views can be expressed
and decisions can be made. Such arenas can be seen as examples of global
civil society. The Framework Convention on Tobacco Control provides an
illustration of what this may mean in concrete terms. In 1999, the World
Health Assembly started a process for adopting a global convention on
tobacco control. An International Negotiating Body was set up to facilitate
discussions among the member states of the World Health Organization.
A range of organisations was invited to make submissions on the
Framework Convention on Tobacco Control. These included public health
organisations, women's groups and state tobacco companies. In 2003, an
intergovernmental treaty was signed outlining a regulatory framework for
member states to set out national legislation for tobacco control (Lee 2003).
The process of creating global institutions is unlikely to be easy. One only

has to consider arguments about the democratic legitimacy of supra-state bodies such as the European Parliament to realise that this is not a straightforward matter. Similarly, any attempt to support global co-operation must ensure that these institutions are not dominated by the richest and most powerful nations.

Second, sufficient capacity is needed within the system of provision or supply. If we focus on the choices that users express between different providers, then choice implies that people have a choice of at least two different providers, such as two different schools or hospitals. For choice to exist there has to be an adequate number of providers or, alternatively put, sufficient capacity in the system of supply or provision. A key problem facing the introduction of choice, however, is when sufficient capacity does not exist within public services. In this case, opportunities for users to exercise choice will be curtailed. If providers are able in this situation to select the users that they wish to serve, then the possibility arises that they may engage in 'cream-skimming' or 'cherry-picking'. This means that providers may select the users that they personally find the most attractive or easiest to serve regardless of the needs of individual users. Schools that are oversubscribed may try to select pupils who will generate high marks in public examinations, and hospitals faced with an excess of potential patients may choose to treat those who are cheap to treat. This is problematic because rather than empowering individuals, user choice within tight capacity constraints in the system of provision may mean that certain groups – such as the poor, old and sick – are excluded from popular schools and hospitals. This means that access to public services will not be equitable for all. Some analysts have suggested that trying to implement user choice within tight capacity constraints on the supply side may effectively transform user choice into provider choice (Lent and Arend 2004; Working Commission on Choice in K-12 Education 2004).

A combination of insufficient capacity within the system of provision and the scope for providers to select users opens up the possibility of cream-skimming. Of course, schools and hospitals might try not to serve particular users even though they have not come up against capacity constraints. However, if public services are mandated to serve those who apply to them, then cream-skimming could only emerge once the capacity constraints have been reached. The likelihood can be reduced by alleviating capacity constraints or narrowing the scope for providers to exercise choice. To help cope with extra demand, individual schools or hospitals could be allowed to grow. Although this strategy will help cope with excess demand, this may take time to put into place. If the provider is investing in extra capacity (building extra classes or having more hospital beds), then they cannot accommodate extra demand instantaneously. In addition, they might only add extra capacity once demand has exceeded a certain threshold (enough pupils to fill an extra class say). This is also likely to be costly, which underlines that implementing choice is not a cheap policy option (Perri 6 2003; Lent and Arend 2004; Working Commission on Choice in K-12 Education 2004). Instead of building extra capacity themselves, providers might be able to contract for spare capacity elsewhere. To help ensure sufficient capacity within the system of provision, there is a case for allowing providers to draw on the resources of other providers, both public and private. As well as allowing popular providers to expand, public policy should permit less popular suppliers to contract if necessary. In some cases, the possibility must be faced that a provider may not find it viable to continue operating. Although government should try and avoid this where possible – to help minimise disruption to users – one should accept that introducing choice introduces the possibility of exit.

Even after attempts to expand capacity, demand might still outstrip supply. In this situation, other steps could be taken to help reduce the possibility of cream-skimming. These measures focus on the decisions taken by providers. One option would be for governing authorities to require providers to introduce a lottery system once they become oversubscribed. Thus, places at a school could be allocated by a random draw of those applying to the school (Brighouse 2000). A different option would be to try and introduce incentives for providers to take on people they would otherwise neglect. Hospitals might be able to claim higher payments from government for treatment of high cost patients.

The third aspect of choice is information for users. If user choice is to be fully effective, then this should be made on an informed basis. Individuals should be aware of the options that are available and have data on the performance of different organisations. Although doctors are likely to have access to specialist medical knowledge that is not possessed by users, the arguments considered in Chapter 3 suggest that information asymmetries do not always run one way. They turn the above asymmetries on their head by implying that there are situations in which providers may be much less informed than citizens about the preferences, expectations and interests of users. It is important for providers to be responsive to the changing needs of their users if they are to retain public support and confidence. A problem for providers is that they are likely to face difficulties in directly accessing the knowledge needed to develop a responsive service. This knowledge is dispersed and fragmented throughout society. User choice can play a useful role in revealing this information, because users will gravitate towards features that they regard as desirable. In this way, choice can help services evolve to provide a responsive service (Corry et al. 2003).

It is true that public service professionals have access to specialist knowledge or expertise that is often not easy to communicate to users. Indeed, this knowledge may serve to confuse rather than illuminate people. That said, data on key aspects of performance can be transmitted in a fairly simple format. For instance, schools could publish data related to the performance of their students in examinations in the different subject areas. Similarly, hospitals could make available information related to waiting times for different operations as well as standards of cleanliness. The content of such information is subject to legitimate debate. Carol Propper and Deborah Wilson (2003) point out that the multiple tasks that public services perform mean that it is difficult to rely only on a single performance measure when communicating information to users. A range of performance measures should be adopted. Propper and Wilson argue that any measure should take into account the different inputs or resources associated with different institutions. Hospitals in poorer areas may have greater problems to contend with than those in richer areas (their patients may suffer from worse health and so require more intensive and expensive treatment), and so concentrating on gross performance outcomes is unlikely to give an accurate picture of performance of different hospitals. Attention should focus instead on 'value-added' indicators. Carol Propper and Deborah Wilson say that before implementing a particular measure, it should be subject to careful piloting. As part of this, they say that measures should be based on sources of information that are not easy to manipulate by those whose performance is being assessed. This helps maintain the integrity of the information provided to the public. Propper and Wilson say that independent national surveys could play a role in providing a source of information that is difficult to manipulate by professionals.

Although information is important for helping underpin a system of user choice, one also ought to acknowledge its limitations. First, it may take time to develop adequate sources of information. Although piloting can help improve the quality of information available to the public, an element of learning by doing is likely to be involved. Simon Burgess et al. (2005) argue that although information may be unreliable in the early stages of a choice scheme, it is nevertheless important to publish this data to help support public confidence in choice. Second, there is a danger that professionals will direct time and energy towards those aspects of performance that they are being measured on to the detriment of other worthwhile activities. For example, teachers might concentrate only on teaching pupils the necessary skills and knowledge to pass examinations rather than developing a broader education (Crouch 2003). There is no easy way of resolving this problem. One solution would be to abandon performance measures. The difficulty with this is that information is needed for the exercise of choice. Abandoning choice in favour of voice is not a solution as a system of regulation should be in place whether we emphasise choice or voice, and performance measures are important for regulation.

Voice

As with choice, a range of things should be in place for voice to be fully operational. First, central intervention is needed to help establish and regulate voice. Individuals require a variety of resources in order to exercise voice (Verba et al. 1995; Birchall 2002a). These include the necessary skills to present one's own views and engage in reasoned debate, sufficient time to take part in discussions and access to financial resources (to pay, for example, for childcare while one attends a planning committee). Government can play a role in assisting people to acquire these resources. For example, government could put in place a legal framework that allows employees to take time off from their daily duties to take part in forums such as joint consultative committees.

Central intervention is also likely to be necessary to redress inequalities of power and resources that exist between individuals. Even if it is possible to guarantee that both users and producers have access to adequate resources to engage in voice, it is likely that some people will be in a better position to exercise voice than others. Some people might be more articulate than others. Others might have more time on their hands or have access to greater financial resources. The different resources that people possess raise a problem because it can be a source of domination or inequality (Cohen and Rogers 1995; Fung and Wright 2001; Dixon et al. 2003). People may use their superior resources to help drown out the views of others (Cohen and Rogers 1995). In a system with rationing in the supply of services, the most articulate may be able to push themselves to the front of any queue (Dixon et al. 2003). Central intervention is needed to help protect the interests of those less well placed to exercise voice. This may include the provision of greater resources to such people by the government. Joshua Cohen and Joel Rogers dub such measures 'democratic associationalism', that is the attempt by central authorities to correct inequalities of power and resources within a diverse system of provision.

As well as helping people have access to the resources they need for voice, central authorities have a part to play in regulating the conduct of voice. All organisations are subject to some form of regulation by public authorities. Regulation is concerned with issues of the public interest. This applies just as much to those bodies that pursue profit as to bodies that pursue other objectives. For example, within the private sector, companies require a license to operate from public authorities if they are to exist at all. This license to operate raises issues of the purpose of the organisation, which in turn connects to the realm of the public interest (Parkinson 1993; Gamble 2000; Gamble and Kelly 2000). In the next chapter we shall look at those organisations that have a specific public interest objective built into their internal constitutions. Voice needs to be subject to regulation for a variety of reasons. For example, regulations are important for ensuring that providers have in place an organisational strategy for encouraging voice. Johnston Birchall (2002a) argues that one of the important background conditions for encouraging voice, alongside individuals having the resources to exercise voice as well as the presence of opportunities for voice, is that organisations should have a strategy for supporting participation. This includes the provision of an information rich environment, adequate office space and appropriate expense and training budgets. Central authorities can support this by requiring that organisations have such a strategy. Regulations are also important for protecting the rights of users. For instance, Anna Coote and David Hunter (1996) highlight the significance of procedural rights within health, such as a right of users to be subject to unbiased decision-making by health employees, a right to refer any refusals of service that users experience to an independent review and a right to be provided with reasons for decisions that are taken.

A second issue is about who is allowed to express a voice. In light of the importance of making public services responsive to the views of users, voice should be provided to the users of public services. However, users are not a homogeneous group of individuals. There are different types of users, and different individuals use public services in different ways. For example, within schools, pupils are perhaps the most direct user group. They absorb the lessons provided by their teachers, and have regular and intensive contact with their teachers. Further removed are parents who also use schools. They rely on schools for the education of their children, but often have irregular contact with schools. University admission tutors draw on the pool of pupils provided to them by schools and so are interested in the quality of education provided by schools. In transport, season-ticket holders on railways have regular contact with services provided by trains. Local employers also rely on train services to get their employees to work on time. Elsewhere, tourists may use trains to go on holiday. While all these different user groups may have many things in common, they are also likely to have specific concerns. For instance, local employers may only be interested in the skills that school-leavers have, which are directly relevant to their particular firm, rather than the content of their broader education. Much the same could be said about those who provide public services. The sorts of collective models of knowledge mentioned in the previous chapter emerge from relationships between different types of stakeholders, and these stakeholders include workers as well as the broader public. Differences exist within the workforce, for instance, between general administrative staff and those who have frontline contact with users. In education, differences exist between head-teachers, caretakers, teaching assistants, cleaners and catering employees. In involving stakeholders, a decision has to be made about which particular stakeholders to involve. One might group together all the users and producers and give voice rights to the user and producer groups. Alternatively, we might differentiate between different types of users or producers and only give a say to particular classes of users and producers. Although enhancing voice points to spreading voice rights as widely as possible between, and within, different groups, a trade-off will be faced between providing a space for different voices and increasing the likelihood that decision-making will be clogged up by the plethora of voices. The precise balance will differ between different public services and over different points of time.

Second, it is important to provide appropriate channels for participation. Voice can be shaped in a number of ways (Arnstein 1969; Birchall 2002b; Chen 2003). Sherry Arnstein (1969) provides an influential account of the different facets of voice in her analysis of a 'ladder of participation'. Arnstein was interested in charting the different ways that citizens could be involved within public services. She outlines an eightfold typology that forms her ladder of participation. She calls the first and lowest rung of the ladder of participation 'manipulation'. She says that this involves citizens being subject to rubber-stamping committees. Public authorities have already made decisions, and users have little scope for influencing the decisions or actions of these bodies. As an example of this, she highlights the part played by Citizen Action Committees (CACs) within urban renewal in the United States. She says that while CACs were intended to provide minority communities such as African–Americans with a voice in the operation of city housing schemes, in practice, council officials saw these bodies as a way to engineer their own perspectives. The second rung of participation is called therapy. People are brought into collective forums, but are subject to collective group therapy so that citizens are 'educated' to adopt particular policy positions. The third rung is the provision of information. In this mode, citizens are provided with information about their respective rights and responsibilities. Arnstein argues, however, that the flow of information here is predominantly one way, from officials to the public. The fourth rung involves consultation. Users are consulted about their views on various policy options and invited to express their views. The fifth rung is placation, whereby a few handpicked worthies are allowed to operate on the boards of public bodies. As users are placed in a minority on such boards, however, they are easy to placate or override. The sixth rung is partnership, whereby users and officials share decision-making responsibilities through institutions such as joint policy boards and planning committees. The seventh rung consists of delegated power where citizens have a dominant authority over a particular policy area, for example gained by citizens having a majority of seats on the boards of public bodies. The eighth rung comprises of citizen control, where citizens have overall control of the decisions and actions made by a particular body. Sherry Arnstein notes that the level of citizen involvement rises with the height of the ladder. In fact, she argues that only the sixth, seventh and eight rungs (partnership, delegated power and citizen control) correspond to genuine participation by users. She says that although the third, fourth and fifth rungs (information, consultation and placation) contain the seeds of participation, in effect they add up to token involvement of users within public bodies. She continues that the first and second rungs (manipulation and therapy) in effect amount to non-participation. Although Arnstein's typology can be modified and extended in various ways, it nevertheless provides an overview of the main channels for exercising voice.

While we might agree with Arnstein that one ought to try and get as high up the ladder of participation as possible, implementing an effective channel for voice may mean that one has to settle for one of the lower rungs. One factor influencing the choice of rung relates to the likelihood that a user will use the channel provided. Johnston Birchall and Richard Simmons have elaborated and empirically tested a model of user participation within public services (Birchall 2002a, 2002b; Birchall and Simmons 2002). Based on this, Birchall and Simmons contend that the likelihood of user participation within public services depends importantly on the character of the relationships that users enjoy with public services. They argue that there are four elements to such relationships. First, the continuity of need charts whether the needs that users face is occasional or more long lasting. The more continuous a person's need, the greater the likelihood that they will participate within public services. Second, the intensity of need maps out how intense is the need felt by users. They say that intensity varies from situations where the need the user faces is relatively frivolous to one where this need is lifesaving. Birchall and Simmons argue that greater intensity of need spurs greater participation. Third, the level of financial involvement sets out how much of the user's own financial resources are invested in the relationship between user and producer. The more a person has invested financially in a public service, the more likely they are to want to take part within these public services. Fourth, the degree of competence indicates how competent users are in assessing the product or service. Greater competence is a motor behind greater activity.

This model of user participation helps predict which channels are likely to be effective under what circumstances. Within health, the relationship of a patient to a hospital is often intermittent or occasional in character. The intermittent nature of the relationship is partially offset by the fact that the need the patient feels may be intense in character. Individuals usually find themselves relying on the professional expertise of doctors and nurses, and the patients often have a low level of financial involvement within health services. From this we would predict that it is difficult to organise participation within health. This means that the higher rungs of Arnstein's ladder may not yield much in the way of participation. Within education, parents enjoy a high degree of continuity with schools during the period of compulsory schooling for their children. Parents are usually intensely interested in the education of their children, but (as in health) do not typically have a high degree of financial involvement with schools. Parents are likely to be competent to assess school results. We would predict that there is a greater chance of participation within education than health, and so one can move up the ladder of participation. Participation is more likely within transport than either health or education for certain categories of passengers. Season-ticket holders have continuous relations with providers. They are often intensely interested in performance (over issues such as punctuality), and their season tickets mean that they have a high degree of financial involvement in the service. Finally, passengers can assess fairly easily the quality of service delivered. Here the possibility exists that channels such as partnership may be able to yield active involvement by citizens.

Public service professionals

Up to now, this book has focused largely on analysing public services from the perspective of those who use such services. However, creating opportunities for greater user choice and voice within areas such as health and education will impact on professionals who provide these services. Doctors may receive increasing calls from users to administer particular types of treatment or have access to specific types of medical technology. Teachers will have to cope with the need to attract sufficient numbers of students. The reaction of professionals to attempts to promote user participation is important because public services typically rely heavily on the actions of their staff, that is they are 'labour-intensive' (Prentice 2002; Ironside and Seifert 2004). Doctors, nurses, radiographers and paramedics are all crucial to the successful operation of health services. Likewise, schools could not operate without the input of teachers or classroom assistants. The success of a diverse system of provision depends therefore on securing the support of its employees.

A public service ethos has often been ascribed to public sector employees. Raymond Plant (2003) contends that this public service ethic is composed of a number of components that includes service, professionalism and impartiality. Service means that public servants are motivated by commitment to the common good rather than self-interest. Professionalism implies that workers have access to knowledge that is not widely available. Doctors, for example, have access to medical knowledge about illnesses and cures that are not usually available to the general population. Impartiality means that the rules regarding delivery are implemented in a disinterested way. Evidence exists which supports the idea that public servants are motivated in important part by an ethic of public service. To test for the existence of public service motivations, Gene Brewer and Sally Coleman Selden (1998) conducted an empirical study of 'whistle blowing' in the federal civil service in the United States. They contend that whistle blowing is an important behaviour because it can have major implications for organisational change. They hypothesise that while whistle blowing is fuelled by a number of factors, there is a link between a service ethic and whistle blowing. This is because whistle blowing has an element of self-sacrifice and is motivated importantly by conscience and responsibility. To test this, they used data from the 1992 Merit Principles Survey collected by the United States Merit Systems Protection board. This survey involved a sample of 20,851 full-time employees in the federal government. Around 13,400 staff returned completed questionnaires (a response rate of around 64 per cent). In their study, Brewer and Coleman Selden sampled 2188 employees who said they had personally seen or obtained direct evidence of illegal activities involving their employers. About 51.4 per cent of these employees said they reported this activity. Using statistical methods, Brewer and Coleman

Selden found that the data backed their initial theory, that whistle blowers are motivated mainly by a concern with the public interest. Moreover, rather than being disgruntled employees, many of these workers had high levels of achievement, job commitment and satisfaction. Elsewhere, Philip Crewson (1997) conducted statistical analysis on data in the United States from the General Social Survey, the 1979 Federal Employee Attitude Survey and the 1994 member survey of electrical engineers to test for the incidence and consistency over time of public service motivations. He discovered that public sector employees had different expectations and motivations than private sector counterparts and that profit-seeking firms are likely to be dominated by economically oriented staff, while public service bodies are dominated by service-oriented individuals.

Professionals will probably view important parts of an agenda to promote user participation in a positive light. Implementing user voice and choice will imply an important degree of professional autonomy. In a system of choice, staff should be in a position to tailor their services and be responsive to the shifting expectations of users. Professionals will need to be autonomous in order to deliver this level of responsiveness. Similarly, I have noted that moves to create organisational knowledge imply a role for producers as well as users, and this means granting employees voice rights and so some professional autonomy. In general, staff are likely to respond positively to these features. Professionals probably place a high value on autonomy within their working lives. Being subject to extensive control by central authorities is likely to sap morale and constitute a source of dissatisfaction. Consequently, a system that opens up the potential for autonomy will probably be welcomed by many producers.

As well as opening up the choices available to users, a diverse system of provision will create choices for workers. Individuals will be able to choose from a varied mix of employers. Timothy Besley and Maitreesh Ghatak (2003) argue that choice can act as a useful mechanism for matching employees to employers. Besley and Ghatak argue that individuals work harder for an organisation if they agree with its goals. They continue that most workers within public services want to work for bodies that strive for a 'mission'. A mission is understood to encompass a service objective and differs from profit in the federal government. Besley and Ghatak say that organisations will pursue different missions and that different workers will value different missions. They argue that productivity is maximised when workers are matched to the organisations whose missions they value. Besley and Ghatak suggest that competition offers the best way of matching workers and providers who are dispersed throughout the country.

This is not to say producers will see a plural model of public services as an unalloyed good. Producers are likely to prefer a system in which they have complete control over decision-making over one in which they have to share decision-making with others. This might not matter much if producers and users would come to the same sorts of decisions within public services. However, one of the insights of public choice theory is that different people have different interests, and these interests can collide. One can subscribe to this without also believing that individuals are driven simply by personal gain. Users and producers might have different views about how resources are distributed within public services, and these differences can yield conflicts and tensions. For example, a doctor might not wish to administer expensive treatment to a sick individual who the doctor feels has little chance of survival. The patient's family, however, might demand such treatment if there is a slight possibility that this will prolong the patient's life. At a much broader level, staff will have to engage more directly with users, and a substantial proportion may feel that this is an unnecessary distraction. David Chan and Lee Gan Goh (2000) provide some evidence of the concerns that doctors have over patient autonomy. Based on a survey conducted in Singapore between December 1997 and March 1998 that was completed by 249 doctors (135 general practitioners and 114 medical specialists) out of a sample of 475 doctors, Chan and Gan Goh found that while doctors believed that patients were more knowledgeable about medicine than ten years ago (this view was expressed by 89 per cent of general practitioners and 86 per cent of medical specialists), around two-thirds of all doctors believe that patients are seldom, often or usually incapable of making rational healthcare choices. Furthermore, if a patient refuses treatment around 80 per cent of doctors try to circumvent this by getting themselves or the patient's family to try and persuade the patient to accept the treatment.

The overall attitude of professionals to the version of public service is likely to be mixed. While workers will probably welcome some aspects, they may be unhappy about others. Of course, the attitudes of workers towards any system of public services are likely to be mixed. Under a centralised model, professionals may not have to engage in discussion with users but do not experience much in the way of professional autonomy. Under a version that emphasises free markets, the experience of professional autonomy may co-exist with worries about adequate levels of funding for public service. The fact that the reaction of professionals is likely to be mixed does not on its own undermine the case for a plural system of provision. The issue rather is whether a plural system performs better or worse than other ways of organising public services. At this stage, we do not have sufficient evidence to make this judgement, in part because features such as user choice are still at a fairly early stage of development. Until this happens, a few remarks about the possible ways of dealing with the sorts of concerns mentioned about may be in order. While it is unlikely that concerns will disappear, the below should hopefully outline a partial redress of these issues.

The arguments of this book support the participation of users within public services. This means that professionals will have to engage with users on some level. The widespread application of paternalism, where professionals make all decisions on behalf of users, is not an option. The task is to try and negotiate some of the inevitable tensions that will arise between the public servant and user. This relationship can be fashioned in a variety of ways. Timothy Quill and Howard Brody (1996) argue that one possibility is for professionals to place all decision-making power in the hands of users. They say that within health this means doctors refraining from making choices and leaving it to patients to make policy decisions. Quill and Brody contend that this model of the doctor–patient relationship is problematic because it does not allow the doctor to draw on their experience to allow the patient to make informed decisions. Quill and Brody advocate instead a model of 'enhanced autonomy' in which doctors provide information about the policy choices available but then allow patients to make decisions (see also Chin 2002; Coulter 2002; Faller 2003). The idea of enhanced autonomy offers a way that doctors, and more generally professionals, address the perceived difficulties of users making choices on their own. Of course, this process is not easy. Doctors may feel overwhelmed by patients arriving at consultations with masses of information downloaded from the Internet. Furthermore, professionals may feel that patients are still incapable of making proper choices even after having discussed the various options on offer. While enhanced autonomy is not without problems, it offers an avenue down which professionals can respect the autonomy of users, while also allowing their professional experience to have a bearing on the decisions that users make.

Conclusion

This chapter has looked at some of the features that need to be in place in order to help establish a system of user activity. Broadly speaking, it set out a general framework in which providers experience local autonomy within a framework of centrally defined standards. Of course, such a system is not without tensions. The centre can become overbearing and stifle the autonomy of local providers. While such an approach is not without problems, a focus on standards and local autonomy potentially lays the ground for active user involvement while trying to protect the standards of service experienced by users and public servants alike. The next chapter continues this examination, by looking more closely on what such an approach may amount to in concrete terms.

5 The Public Interest Company

Introduction

In Chapter 4, I set out the general shape of the version of public services put forward in this book. Briefly put, the general framework is of a range of suppliers providing services within a framework of centrally defined standards. These providers allow for sufficient opportunities for users to exercise both voice and choice. This chapter looks at this issue in more detail, homing in more closely on what this framework will mean in practical institutional terms. The chapter discusses the institutional form that exemplifies the commitment to central standards and local autonomy, the 'public interest company' or 'public benefit corporation'. The public interest company embodies the broad version of public services set out here in two main ways. First, the corporate or company form of these institutions highlights the freedoms enjoyed from central government. Second, the commitment to the public interest or public benefit nevertheless indicates that these organisations have to operate within a framework of central standards. Although diversity within provision means that no single form is suitable across all contexts, the public interest company form helps capture the commitment to local autonomy and central standards.

Public interest companies already exist in different parts of the world. For example, in the United States, the Metropolitan Transport Authority (MTA) is a public benefit corporation. This organisation provides rail, bus and tube services for New York City, Long Island, southeastern New York State and Connecticut. This is North America's largest transport network, serving 14.6 million people. The MTA draws funds from federal, state and local government sources and issues debt. This body was provided with a public benefit corporation charter in 1965 and is governed by a 17-member board. Members are nominated by the Governor of New York, with recommendations made by New York City's Mayor and officials from Nassau, Suffolk, Westchester, Dutchess, Orange, Rockland and Putnam counties (the latter four counries cast one collective vote). The board also has six rotating members held by employee representatives and the Permanent Citizens Advisory Committee (PCAC). In Australia, an Indigenous Land Corporation (ILC) was established in 1995 to help indigenous people acquire and manage land throughout Australia. The ILC has a seven-member board, which is selected by the Minister for Immigration and Multicultural and Indigenous Affairs. The Chairperson and at least four other members must be indigenous. Up to 2004, funds came from a Land Fund, which received a fixed annual allocation of Au $121 million Australian dollars (index linked) from the government. About two-thirds of this money has been retained and invested, and as of 30 June 2004, the Land Fund was worth around 1.3 billion Australian dollars. Government contributions ceased in 2004, and the ILC uses investment income to fund its activities.

There is already a literature on these and other types of 'hybrid' bodies that go beyond traditional public enterprise and for-profit private companies. This occurs, for instance, in the work of students of American public administration such as Philip Selznick (1953) and his work on the Tennessee Valley Authority, Harold Seidman (1952, 1954) and his researches into the government corporation and Jonathan Koppell's (2003) exploration of quasi-government. Although there has been scholarly attention to these bodies, much remains to be explored about these bodies. In his recent survey, Jonathan Koppell states that these bodies have not attracted the attention they deserve. He records a 'lack of popular or scholarly attention' (Koppell 2003, 2) towards these bodies and that 'Despite their popularity and importance, hybrids have not received much attention' (Koppell 2003, 8). There is, however, growing attention to these types of organisation. Paul Maltby writes that in,

> last year the debate about the best way to deliver public services has stumbled on a new option – a not-for-profit company, or 'public interest company' (PICs). From Network Rail, National Air Traffic Services and Foundation Hospitals, there has been much political and media attention towards those 'new' organisational forms (Maltby 2003b, 2).

This chapter considers the constitution of public interest companies, looking in particular at how these bodies may be designed to foster the involvement of users and employees within the health sector. In the first section of the chapter, I outline the main elements of the public interest company, drawing on a detailed definition outlined recently by the Public Management Foundation. I then apply the public interest company model within the realm of health, examining the constitution of foundation hospitals. I look at health because of the importance of this sector within public services in general as well as the fact that the foundation hospital model has already emerged across different parts of the world. Jonathan Koppell (2003) highlights the importance of considering how hybrid organisations are constituted in his analysis of the problems that hybrids raise for traditional bureaucratic control. In particular, he says that central authorities face problems in controlling the actions of hybrid organisations. An agency problem exists whereby the injunction of the hybrid organisation to pursue a social policy goal may come into conflict with one of the organisation's own objectives. Koppell argues that the most obvious instance of this occurs when a commitment to achieve a social policy goal conflicts with an organisational goal to maximise profits. Koppell contends that central authorities face a greater problem in controlling the activities of providers in situations in which provision is through hybrid organisations rather than a centralised bureaucracy. Koppell continues that the presence of this control problem does not necessarily undermine the case for hybrids. He says that hybrids could nevertheless be justified on some other basis, such as the opportunities that these organisations offer for improving the responsiveness of public services to their users. He adds though that in this case research ought to demonstrate that hybrids will in fact improve responsiveness. However, as yet, further work is needed on such issues. Koppell writes that there is,

> no reason that hybrids cannot be accountable in the responsibility or responsiveness senses as here defined. In order for these types of accountability to prove meaningful substitutes for control, however, the public objectives of the hybrid organization must be translated into the language of responsibility or responsiveness. As the discussion above indicates, this is a challenging project (Koppell 2003, 183).

Koppell's analysis of hybrids does not match exactly the public interest company model set out here. The public interest company set out here does not allow dividend payments to be made to stakeholders from the surplus generated by the organisation, whereas in Koppell's analysis hybrids do permit dividend payments. While differences do exist, Koppell identifies issues relevant for this study. Public interest companies are presented as a way of promoting user involvement. Given this injunction, an obvious issue relates to how these bodies might be designed to promote user involvement.

This chapter considers how foundation hospitals might be designed to allow the active involvement of individuals within these institutions. This discussion is conducted at the theoretical level and therefore does not provide conclusive proof that the policies discussed below will overcome problems of engaging users within hospitals. Empirical evidence is important for arriving at such judgements and as yet sufficient data on such issues is unavailable. In part, as Jonathan Koppell points out, this is because hybrids have not attracted the attention they warrant. In part, this is also because the specific ideas here need to be tested empirically. Although it is important to gather data on these issues, a necessary preliminary is to sketch out the ways that hospitals might be designed to promote user involvement.

What are public interest companies?

The Public Management Foundation is a useful starting point for examining public interest companies because they offer one of the most detailed accounts of these bodies. Nine features are associated with this definition. First, these are organisations charged with acting in the public interest. Paul Corrigan and Jane Steele state that the 'organisation must be seen as one that aims for a public good and not one that creates a profit for shareholders or directors out of that public good' (Corrigan and Steele 2001a, p. 17). Second, the organisation should remain committed to the public benefit over time. The intention of this is to prevent the body from being taken over by another institution that changes it so that it no longer delivers services geared towards the public good. Third, public interest companies should be allowed to trade. Charles Brecher says that this aspect of the definition means that a 'PIC must earn its revenues by exchanging its services for money' (Brecher 2002, 6). Brecher argues that although trading does not mean that public interest companies have to compete with each other or other types of bodies, competition is often useful for helping achieve the fourth and fifth elements of the Public Management Foundation definition of public interest companies. The fourth aspect is that public interest companies should promote cost-efficiency, while the fifth dimension is that managers of these organisations should be encouraged to be entrepreneurial. Brecher suggests that the threat of being undercut by a competitor encourages managers to deliver services as cost-efficiently as possible. Sixth, this organisation is not allowed to make any dividend payments. Any surpluses generated must be reinvested back in the company. Seventh, the public interest company can raise capital from money markets. The aim of this is to use funds raised to promote innovation. Eighth, the organisation should be accountable to different stakeholders. Accountability could encompass stakeholder representation on company boards as well as different types of election appointment for different directors. Ninth, the body should be independent of direct political control from government (Corrigan and Steele 2001a).

Charles Brecher (2002) argues that applying this framework to underground transport services means, first, that the company running the tube would be committed to providing mass transit services. Second, the organisation would be prevented from transferring its assets in other ways in the future. Third, the public interest company would earn the bulk of its revenues through the tickets it sells to travellers. Brecher contends that the setting of fares makes the company a trading organisation. Brecher accepts that while the extent to which the underground could be made a cost-efficient and entrepreneurial organisation (features four and five of the Public Management Foundation definition) is debatable, appropriate design could simulate these characteristics. He says that although the public interest company has a monopoly within the underground, it would compete with alternative types of travel (in particular buses and cars). He adds that the tube could also be subject to various performance indicators imposed from government. These could include a requirement to undertake technical innovations (such as advanced signalling systems) and an injunction to reduce cost per passenger. Sixth, the company would be a not-for-profit body with no shareholders and no possibility for distributing profits to any individuals. Seventh, the revenues that the corporation earns would help it raise additional debt finance from capital markets. Fares will help service the debt that is taken on. Eighth, the board would be composed of stakeholders including leaders of unions representing tube workers, professional safety or engineering organisations, appointees from the government, and large employers in the region. Underground customers could also elect a board member. Last, the composition of the board would help ensure that the firm is independent of central government control.

It is arguable whether the definition outlined by the Public Management Foundation captures all that is relevant about public interest companies. No mention is made, for example, of the view implicit in much of the debate surrounding public interest companies that they should guarantee a prescribed level of service. This commitment is intended to reassure users that a shift from traditional public enterprise will not result in a cut in the quality of the services they experience. Public interest companies are usually seen by its advocates as ushering in a system of local ownership of public services. Local ownership implies the existence of a range of providers. Variations in the level of service are likely to emerge between the different providers (reflecting, for example, differences in local conditions). To protect the quality of service experienced by users in this diverse system of provision, there is the suggestion that all providers have to guarantee a minimum level of service. The principles outlined by the Public Management Foundation are also not always in harmony. For example, in certain situations the requirement to consult with, and involve, stakeholders may help inflate rather than reduce costs. The injunction to be cost-efficient might also threaten the promise that these organisations deliver a prescribed level of service if these efficiencies are achieved by providing lower quality, but less costly, services. Although the definition advanced by the Public Management Foundation is not without tension, it nevertheless provides a valuable and influential account of the basic features of the public interest company model.

Types of public interest company

While the above definition helps pin down the central features of public interest companies, it nonetheless is broad enough to admit a range of different organisational forms. One feature worth noting relates to the different ownership bases of public interest companies. Some models of public interest companies are owned wholly by the state. These nationalised industries have a precedent in the sort of 'public corporation' witnessed in the post-war period. Leonard Tivey argues that individuals such as Herbert Morrison posited a model of public corporations in which industries would be wholly publicly owned and yet the managers of these industries would be independent of direct political control (Tivey 1978). Most of the current versions of public interest companies are not examples of nationalisation. Paul Maltby sets his model of public interest companies in an intermediate position on a 'public service continuum' running from nationalised industries at one end of the spectrum to private companies at the other end (Maltby 2003a, b). This version of public interest companies differs from nationalisation because it does not suggest that these organisations be owned wholly by the state. They also differ from private companies in at least two important respects. First, they do not conceive the public interest in terms of the pursuit of profit. Second, public interest companies do not permit dividend payments. As such shareholders are not a part of the governance structures of these organisations. This introduces a difference with those private firms that do not simply pursue profit (because these private firms do still allow dividend payments). Contemporary models of the public interest company open up an ownership agenda beyond private or state ownership, embracing local forms of public ownership.

A third way in public services?

If we understand state-centred approaches to cover those situations where the state funds and delivers welfare services, then public interest companies differ from traditional public enterprise because they do not rely on the state to deliver welfare services. Insofar as these bodies rely on the state, however, for the main source of funding, then these institutions are not entirely free of state intervention. The existence of market failure within the welfare arena means that there may be little alternative to relying on state finance if services are to be provided to all the citizens of a nation. The sort of state involvement in public interest companies implied here is however substantially different from that experienced under the welfare state. They point to a new ownership agenda, one that focuses on local rather than state ownership. These entities are not, however, a neoliberal model of the firm. Neoliberal conceptions of the firm emphasise the importance of maximising shareholder value (Hart 1995). Because public interest companies do not have a role for dividend payments, the issue of shareholder value does not arise for these organisations.

A possible objection to my argument takes issue with the stability of these organisations. Neoliberals such as Elaine Sternberg suggest that stakeholder models of a firm are unworkable. If true, this means that public interest companies do not produce a stable or viable concept of the third way within public services. Sternberg claims that,

> it is an essential principle of stakeholder theory that corporations should be equally accountable to all their stakeholders. This doctrine is, however, not only wholly unjustified, but also unworkable. An organisation that is accountable to everyone is actually accountable to no-one: accountability that is diffuse, is effectively non-existent. Multiple accountability can only function if everyone involved accepts a clear common purpose. But that is what stakeholder theory conspicuously rejects (Sternberg 1998, 98).

My argument is that although Sternberg raises issues that should not be ignored, her case against stakeholding is exaggerated. Doubts can be expressed at a theoretical level over the arguments she raises (although I acknowledge that this matter may only be settled ultimately at an empirical level once sufficient data on the operations of public interest companies has accumulated). Sternberg makes at least two important claims in her statement above. The first relates to whom managers should be accountable to, that is, which people or groups are thought to be stakeholders. She argues that stakeholders are usually seen as all those who affect or are affected by a corporation. A key problem is that this understanding can be stretched so that virtually everyone can be presented as a stakeholder. She writes that since 'stakeholders are all those who can affect or are affected by the organisation, the number of people whose benefits need to be taken into account is infinite' (Sternberg 1998, 96). Managers will find it impossible to reach decisions that satisfy all stakeholders because of the sheer numbers involved. Stakeholding is a recipe for managerial paralysis.

If stakeholding means that managers have to take everyone into account, then there are grounds to believe that public interest companies will be unworkable. However, stakeholding does not have to take everyone into account. While some understandings of stakeholding may be elastic, not all are. Some advocates of stakeholding, for example, use the arguments that neoliberals often use to support a focus on shareholders to justify other stakeholder claims. Margaret Blair, for example, argues that shareholders are often seen as rightful owners within a firm because of the risk they face as a result of the financial capital they invest in a firm (Blair 1995). Gavin Kelly and John Parkinson contend, however, that the same risk-based arguments also apply to other stakeholders. They say that employees also face risk because of the human capital they invest in a company. Workers in fact may face greater levels of risk because unlike shareholders they are generally unable to diversify this risk by making investments in different companies. Kelly and Parkinson use these arguments to contend that employees, customers and supplier firms have claims just as important as shareholders (Kelly and Parkinson 2001). Models such as these do broaden out the individuals that managers have to consider, but do not stretch the meaning of stakeholding to cover everyone. Managers are unlikely, thus, to be overwhelmed by the numbers of stakeholders they have to consider. It is true that the cut-off point for those to be considered stakeholders is not easy to fix. However, these difficulties apply to all systems of corporate governance, including those that restrict their attention to shareholders. It is likely that those denied stakeholder status would lobby managers to be viewed as stakeholders. This feature is not unique to stakeholding and also applies to those excluded from shareholder models of the firm. It is not clear that the problems faced by stakeholding will be any worse than those endured by shareholder models.

The second claim that Sternberg makes concerns an alleged dilution of accountability that results from broadening the focus on analysis beyond shareholders. She says that accountability can only function well when those to whom the managers are accountable to agree on what ought to be the purpose of corporate policy. For the neoliberal firm, this is usually assumed to be profit. Sternberg suggests that the stakeholder model fractures this single clear purpose. Different stakeholders value different ends. Rather than being subject to some overriding organisational goal, managers have to balance stakeholder benefits. As managers cannot be judged against a single purpose, they are effectively accountable to no one. Stakeholding destroys a sense of accountability. Even if we grant Sternberg's assumption that accountability depends on a single clear purpose, it is not clear why public interest companies would destroy accountability. Public interest companies could be charged with meeting a clear purpose, delivering a specified level of service. Of course, the best way in which this may be achieved may be the subject of considerable debate. But this applies equally to what policies firms have to follow in order to maximise profits.

Elaine Sternberg's view that stakeholding is unworkable ought to be rejected. However, even if one is unconvinced of this judgement and wants to maintain that governance within a firm has to be confined to one category of individuals if it is to function properly, it is not clear why this category has to revolve around shareholders. John Kay, for example, has outlined a model of corporations that place the needs of customers first. Kay argues that market failure in certain industries mandates the need for public intervention. The water industry, for example, displays the conditions of a natural monopoly with little prospect for competition. He says that there is a case for regulation of the water industry to prevent the monopoly provider from abusing its position to exploit consumers. Kay rejects the idea that the state should manage water provision for the sorts of reasons given above. The best way to regulate the provision of water is to build delivery around 'customer corporations'. The water industry would be divided up into separate companies. Managers of these companies would be responsible only to customers (Kay 1996). Even if we accept Sternberg's own assumptions, these customer corporations do constitute a viable third way between traditional public enterprise and for-profit firms.

Foundation hospitals

We have so far looked at the general features of the public interest company and defended the idea that they constitute a third way in public services. I now consider the model applied to a particular policy area. I do this to help give the discussion some concreteness, showing what it might imply in practical terms. I look at the public interest company model in relation to health, that is, so-called foundation hospitals. I concentrate on health for several reasons. First, this is one of the most significant areas of the public services. If we take spending on health as a sign of its importance, then it is clear that across the OECD health is a major area of public policy. Using figures for 2002, health spending as a percentage of gross domestic product ranges from 5.7 per cent in the Slovak Republic to 14.6 per cent in the United States. Public expenditure on health as a proportion of total public spending varies from 10.5 per cent in Austria to 18.4 per cent in the United States (Organization for Economic Co-operation and Development 2004a). Second, there are probably more difficulties in encouraging the involvement of users within health than in any other area of the public services. The model of user motivation put forward by Johnston Birchall and Richard Simmons that was discussed in Chapter 4 predicts that fostering the involvement of users within health is likely to be particularly difficult. Furthermore, health is the sector in which users are more likely to have to rely on the specialist knowledge of professionals than anywhere else in the public services. These obstacles make health an interesting area to study. If institutions within health can be designed to support the active involvement of users, then we can be confident about promoting participation elsewhere (where obstacles are fewer and less intense). Third, health is a realm in which the public interest company is increasingly applied in many parts of the world. In the United States, the public benefit corporation is a central feature of the medical care provided by Kaiser Permanente. This is a California-based health organisation that operates in nine states (California, Colorado, Georgia, Hawaii, Maryland, Ohio, Oregon, Virginia and Washington) as well as in Washington DC. Kaiser Permanente is the United State's largest non-profit health plan and has around 8.2 million members most of whom join through their employers. This organisation has a contracting (Kaiser Foundation Health Plan) and provider (Kaiser Foundation Hospital) wing. Both of these are constituted as public benefit corporations, and Kaiser Permanente has 30 hospitals and 136,407 employees. Elsewhere in the United States, Erie County Medical Center (ECMC) which provides medical care to western New York residents regardless of ability to pay was constituted as a public benefit corporation in July 2003. ECMC has more than 2700 employees and houses community-based health centres, an academic medical centre with 550 in-patient beds and an Erie County Home which has a 638-bed nursing facility. The ECMC Corporation is authorised to set fees, purchase equipment and contract with other providers. It contains a 15-strong voting board, with eight directors appointed by the local governor and seven by Erie County Executive.

In 1994, the Danish Parliament created the Copenhagen Hospital Corporation. The Copenhagen Hospital Corporation combines seven hospitals previously owned by the state and two municipalities within Copenhagen.

This organisation is a public organisation that has three main functions: provide hospital services for the Copenhagen and Frederiksberg municipalities, offer specialist services for the nation and develop as a centre for scientific research. This corporation provides roughly 20 per cent of Danish hospital services, employing around 20,000 staff and providing 4500 beds. The Copenhagen Hospital Corporation is headed by a Council of 15 members. Copenhagen city nominates seven politicians to serve as members, Frederiksberg city nominates two politicians, the state picks two civil servants and four individuals are drawn from the private sector.

In Britain, the first ten foundation hospitals were introduced into the National Health Service (NHS) in April 2004. Foundation hospitals are selected from the pool of best-performing '3 star' hospitals and are based on a public benefit corporation model. These hospitals have a multi-stakeholder membership base drawn from the population served by the hospital (the public constituency) people who have attended the hospital as a patient or a carer of a patient within a time period specified by the constitution (the patient constituency) and those who have an employment contract with the hospital (the staff constituency). In addition, membership rights are provided to those who perform functions for the hospital other than under an employment contract. This category includes those who belong to a Primary Care Trust, local authority or authorities, or a university whose dental or medical schools are affiliated to the hospital. The public and patient constituencies are responsible for choosing more than half of the governors of these hospitals. The staff constituency chooses at least three members of the board of governors, and Primary Care Trust, local authority and university each choose at least one of the governors. Furthermore, a body seen as a partnership organisation within the hospital's constitution may also choose a member of the board. No members of the foundation trust have rights over the surplus generated by the hospital. The public, patient and staff constituency each elect their representatives on the board of governors. The Primary Care Trust, local authority or authorities, university and partner organisations each appoint their own representative on the board of governors. Governors serve three-year terms and are allowed to stand for office again once their term ends.

Membership

It is clear from the above that foundation hospitals can be shaped in a wide variety of ways. I now consider arguments that impinge on how foundation hospitals should be constituted. Following Johnston Birchall (2002b), it is useful to start by considering the appropriate membership base of these hospitals. As in public services, more generally, it is useful to distinguish between those who produce and those who use services. Hospitals rely on the actions of a wide range of staff to operate. These include call-handling staff and receptionists who are usually the first point of contact for patients, ambulance-drivers and porters who transport people to, and within, the hospital and doctors and nurses who provide specialist services. All of these have a direct interest in hospital performance as their employment conditions (such as pay and career prospects) depend on this performance. I believe that if a hospital is to provide a good service, then it is valuable to elicit the views of those who provide that service. They can help identify the features that help or hinder good performance. While it might be true that many workers may prefer to focus on their professional duties rather than being drawn into a broader administrative or governance role, the impact that governance and administration will have on their professional duties means that it is useful for workers to have some say in how hospitals are governed. For example, one governance issue concerns how resources are distributed throughout an organisation (for instance, how resources should be divided among staff wages, medical technology or building works) and the manner in which monies are allocated will affect how doctors, porters and ambulance staff do their jobs. In light of the different types of employees, I think it is valuable to canvas as broad a range of opinion as possible. Of course, there should be limits on how far this is pursued. Where the differences between different groups are minor, there is value in combining these different groups. One distinction worth making, perhaps, is between clinical and non-clinical staff. Significant differences are likely to exist between those staff that rely on a specialist medical knowledge as part of their job and those who perform a more general administrative role. Although both play a valuable role, they are likely to express different views over issues such as the proper scope for public participation in clinical decisions and how best to transfer patients within the hospital.

Although individual employees are key to the provision of services, institutions are also likely to play a significant role in the delivery of healthcare. A university medical or dental school may provide regular specialist services to the hospital or be a source of innovation in medical technology. I believe there is merit in developing some supply chains, allowing a role for these institutions in the governance of these hospitals. This may act as a channel for the transmission of 'know-how' from the organisation producing medical technology as well as offering a forum for hospital employees to share their priorities and concerns.

One option for foundation hospitals is to only provide membership rights to employees. In this case, hospitals would be a producer-led organisation and, on some versions could be based on a workers' co-operative model. In emergency situations, it seems reasonable to allow the professional to make decisions. In non-emergency scenarios, however, there is a case for allowing patients to express their views. Even if we wish to insist against this that 'doctor knows best', there are important non-clinical areas in which users have greater knowledge than professionals on what makes a hospital accessible and a good environment. Patients have direct knowledge about the standards of cleanliness they would expect in a hospital and what would ease the process of making appointments. Tapping into this points to allowing a role for patient voice. In addition, if patients are to be 'co-producers' of their healthcare (contributing to this via their diet and exercise regime), then it is useful to allow them an input into how co-production might be best organised.

As with workers, there are different types of users and it is useful to get a broad swathe of opinion. There are grounds for believing that there are important differences in attitudes between those who have and those who have not had recent experience of public services. Consequently, it may be worthwhile to tap into a patient and public constituency (Chen 2003). As with producers, we can go beyond individuals and also consider the role of institutions. Commissioning bodies are an important type of user group. In the sort of pluralistic system of delivery that has been set out in this book, there will be those bodies that provide services and others that will commission services from a multiplicity of providers. Within health, bodies such as local health authorities may be charged with responsibility for commissioning and these institutions are users insofar as they use the services provided by the foundation hospital to deliver healthcare for the local population. It may be useful to allow commissioning bodies a role in foundation hospitals in view of the financial commitment they make to such organisations.

Motivations and agency

The above reflections provide arguments for a 'multi-stakeholder' base for foundation hospitals, comprising of different types of producers and users. If these different constituencies are to take part within the hospital, however, they must be both willing and able to participate. This raises the issue of motivations and capacity. Taking motivations first, we have seen that there are likely to be problems in encouraging the public to participate in hospitals. To recap, for much of the public, the relationship they have with hospitals will be intermittent. For most of the time, the needs of the public will not be intense. Much of the public will not be in a position to assess fully the competence of doctors or nurses. If health services are free at the point of delivery, then the public will have little financial involvement with hospitals. The theory of user participation put forward by Johnston Birchall and Richard Simmons (2002) predicts that the combined effects of the above means there are likely to be difficulties in encouraging members of the public to participate within hospitals. The patient constituency is more likely to participate within the hospital than the public. Patients have a more regular relationship than the broader public, and their needs are likely to be more intense. Of course, we might qualify this last point by saying that beyond a certain level of intensity, participation is likely to wane or even vanish altogether. The chronically sick, for example, may not find it feasible to participate within the governance of the hospital. Although patients are more likely to participate than the public, they are also subject to similar sorts of conditions, and so it may be difficult to motivate patients to play an active role within hospital governance. Commissioning bodies are more likely to participate within foundation hospitals than either patients or the public. The commission conducted by these organisations means that they have a high degree of financial involvement with foundation hospitals. The contracts they enter into help define a fairly continuous relationship with these hospitals. The continuity of this relationship provides commissioning bodies with an incentive to ensure that the hospital is delivering on its promises. The contracts that commissioning bodies conduct means that they are likely to have some competence in judging the actions of professional staff.

Although Johnston Birchall and Richard Simmons (2002) develop a theory of participation in relation to users, I suggest that many of the features they identify offer a useful starting point for thinking about the motivations of workers. For example, it seems reasonable to suppose that the greater the financial stake that a person has in an organisation, the greater their incentive to participate within the organisation. In relation to workers, this assumption underpins one of the key arguments for employee share ownership schemes within the private sector. In particular, the idea is that providing workers with share options offers a way of allowing them to benefit financially from the success of the firm. This provides them with an incentive to be committed to a firm and perhaps to expend more effort within their jobs (Pendleton 1997). Within a foundation hospital, no stakeholder is allowed to receive dividend payments and so this rules out the use of employee share-ownership schemes. However, workers will draw a salary from the hospital and so have a direct financial stake in the hospital. This financial involvement provides employees with an incentive to take part in the governance of the hospital. This may be bolstered by the fairly continuous relationship that many workers enjoy with the hospital. Long-term relationships can help individuals develop a sense of loyalty to an organisation, and this loyalty can underpin the exercise of voice.

Representation

The issue of motivations carries implications for the types of representation that ought to be adopted within hospitals. As we have seen in an earlier chapter, the interests of stakeholders can be represented in a variety of ways. Stakeholders could directly elect a representative to serve on the company board or a person could be appointed by some authority with a brief to represent a particular set of stakeholders. I start from the presumption that the more direct the form of representation that is made available to stakeholders, the greater the opportunity for stakeholders to express voice or exercise control themselves. Insofar as the aim is to provide stakeholders with the maximum opportunity to conduct such functions, emphasis ought to be placed on direct forms of representation. However, one important issue to consider when selecting the type of representation that is made available is whether or not stakeholders are likely to use the particular channel that is provided to them. If they are not, then attention ought to focus on using an alternative form of representation (even if this is a less direct type of representation).

I have argued that there are likely to be difficulties in encouraging patients and the public to participate within foundation hospitals. This means that direct elections may not be the best way representing the interests of patients and the public. Results from the first wave of foundation hospital elections in England provide some backing for this view. As noted above, patients and the public can vote for a representative within English foundation hospitals. There has been low voter registration, however, with only 34,171 patients and local residents out of a pool of around 2 million NHS patients registering in time to vote for the first elections (Carvel 2004). Of course, low voter registration may not simply be due to the difficulties in encouraging the public constituency to participate. Much of the public may be unaware that they were entitled to vote, and this low level of awareness may have fed into low voter registration. While care should be exercised about how the elections are interpreted, there are reasons for supposing that the use of elections may not be the best way of representing patients or the public. One might opt instead for the representation of patients or the public through a members' organisation. Individuals might be allowed a vote at specified intervals on policies and personnel of the members' organisation. The patients' and public's group would be responsible for selecting representatives to work on the board of foundation hospitals. Commissioning bodies have fewer barriers to participation than either the public or patient constituency, and commissioning organisations could be allowed to appoint a representative to serve on foundation hospitals. The choice of representative might have to be ratified by members of the commissioning body through a vote. Workers are more likely to participate than patients or the public, and for staff, direct elections might be a feasible option. For dental or medical schools, there may be a case for using the same sort of representation as that deployed for commissioning organisations.

The public benefit

Having looked at the appropriate membership base of foundation hospitals, as well as the sort of representation that might be deployed within the hospital, I now consider some of the freedoms that might be enjoyed by these hospitals. These freedoms will help define the sorts of rights that the members can exercise. I do not attempt an exhaustive survey of all the freedoms of foundation hospitals, but focus rather on the more important or controversial functions. Johnston Birchall (2002b) highlights that one of the most significant set of rights of any organisation relates to whether or not stakeholders are entitled to the surplus generated by the organisation. Foundation hospitals are supposed to work for the public benefit. This public benefit is likely to consist of a commitment to satisfy the health needs of the local population. In order to protect the public benefit, a 'lock' could be imposed by a regulatory regime on this commitment. This means that a change in management would be unable to change the mission of the hospital. Some observers however, question whether this lock would be enough to stop its mission being changed in all cases. In particular, a range of organisations might apply to the public benefit corporations. While many of these might have operated previously in the state sector, they could also emerge from the realm of voluntary or community organisations, or from the private sector. A private company might establish a subsidiary that operates as a public interest company or could apply to run a foundation hospital that is already set up.

Some argue that allowing the private sector to run foundation hospitals, however, would undermine the commitment to the public benefit. Although private sector firms have a formal commitment to the public benefit, in reality, they would adopt practices that advance the interests of shareholders. This critique rests on the assumption that shareholders are both willing and able to use the foundation hospital as a vehicle for pursuing their own interests. The idea that shareholders will use the public benefit commitment as a mask for their own interests is a species of the public choice critique of the public interest covered in an earlier chapter. I sought to defend the public interest against the charge that it is nothing other than the pursuit of the private interest. This means that if shareholders declare a commitment to the public interest, then this should not be dismissed as automatically being nothing other than empty rhetoric. Shareholder commitment to the public benefit may be genuine. However, even if one believes that shareholders are willing to pursue their private interest, one can question whether they are able to pursue their agenda. This raises the issue of the rights that shareholders exercise over the hospital. The more rights they have over the hospital, the easier it is for them to advance their own interests. This connects to the broader issue of ownership of these hospitals. To analyse this claim I first set out the main facets of ownership. I then consider what is implied by shareholder ownership of firms and whether these ownership rights transfer to foundation hospitals.

A.M. Honoré has set out an influential analysis of the different facets of ownership. According to Honoré, ownership is composed of eleven different components. First, the right of possession implies that the property-owner can insist on holding the object in question for themselves. Second, the right to use means that the property-holder can use the object in any way they please. Third, the right to manage implies that if the property-holder lends the property to another party, they have the right to tell the borrower how to use the item. Fourth, the owner has the right to any income generated from the use of the object. Fifth, the right to capital value implies that the owner has the right to the proceeds generated from the sale of the item. Sixth, the property-holder has a right to be protected from the theft of the property. Seventh, the right of transmission covers the right of the owner to transmit the object to others. This means that the owner could lend the object to another party or offer it as a gift or bequest. Eighth, the rights of freehold mean that no time limits exist over the rights that an owner possesses. Ninth, duty of care implies that the property-holder should not use the object to harm others. Tenth, judgement liability means that the owner is liable for any legal action taken with respect to the object. Finally, the right of residual control means that the person resumes all those rights of ownership they confer to borrowers once the period of the loan is completed (Honoré 1961). 'Pure' forms of ownership (where all rights are allocated to public or private hands) are rare and exist only in relation to the simplest of objects (Gamble and Kelly 1996). As companies do not fall into the category of a simple object, ownership for private corporations is a complex affair. John Kay (1997) argues that when examining the shareholder system of ownership, it is important to make a distinction between the ownership claims that a shareholder has over their shares and the ownership claims they have over the company. He argues that while shareholders can be said to enjoy fully ownership rights over shares, they only have partial rights over the company. In relation to shares, he says shareholders can insist on holding the shares for themselves, use and manage them in any way they please, have rights over the income generated from shares as well as the proceeds of the shares if sold, are protected from the theft of shares, can gift or bequest the shares to others, have freehold over the shares and have a duty to do no harm, are liable for misuse of shares and retain rights of residual control. Kay continues that with respect to firms, shareholders can be said to have unequivocal rights over two aspects of companies. These are the right to exercise residual control over the company, and no time limits on the rights they enjoy (rights eight and eleven on Honoré's framework). He says that shareholders can be said to exercise partial rights over the right to manage the company as they please (right three), the right to an income from the sale of a firm's services (right four) and some rights of the capital value of a corporation if the firm is liquidated (right five). Kay says that shareholders cannot be said to enjoy the rights in other areas. They do not have special rights over use and cannot simply attempt to possess the company. They cannot give away the company and are not properly protected from the expropriation of a firm's assets. They are not held responsible for harmful actions by the company and are not usually held fully liable for a firm's actions. Other parties, such as the directors of the company are the bearers of these rights.

Not all observers agree with Kay's account of the ownership rights enjoyed by shareholders. For example, Ruth Levitas argues that Kay downplays the rights of ownership over the company enjoyed by shareholders (Levitas 1998). For example, we can question whether a shareholder's right to manage is as tenuous as Kay seems to suggest. Shareholders can specify that directors of a firm maximise profits, rather than pursue some corporate social responsibility objective. While Kay's analysis should not be viewed uncritically, it does provide a baseline account of the rights enjoyed by shareholders from someone who leans against exaggerating the rights of shareholders. Having set out the sorts of rights that shareholders enjoy within a shareholder model of the firm, I now examine ownership in relation to foundation hospitals. To start with, shareholders do not enjoy the sorts of rights that John Kay identifies within the shareholder model of the firm. This tends to lie instead with public authorities. The rights that shareholders possess are not time-unlimited, but are rather restricted by the licence to operate granted by regulator (which can be terminated if a foundation hospital is deemed to fail). Shareholders do not have the right to manage the hospital as they please. As noted above, foundation hospitals have to stick to delivering goods and services for the purposes of health. Any sale of services or assets is confined to reinvestment within the hospital, and shareholders have no rights to dividends or capital generated from the hospital. The stakeholder constituency enjoys more rights than that exhibited by shareholders. Although the points about the rights of residual control, freehold and capital value apply equally to stakeholders as they do to shareholders, the former are better placed than the latter at exerting various control rights. While the stakeholders do not enjoy untrammelled rights to manage, all the constituencies have a say in the policies that the trust pursues within the specified realm of freedom from central control. While no stakeholders can receive a dividend payment, all have a right that the whole of the surplus is reinvested on their behalf. In sum, I think there are reasons to doubt whether shareholders enjoy the same rights over a foundation hospital as they do over the parent company, and consequently, they may not be able to influence policy in the manner that Pollock suggests.

Financial freedoms

An important area of financial freedom relates to the flexibility that employers enjoy in setting the pay and conditions of employees. In a system in which the centralised state is the monopoly funder and provider of public services, pay and conditions might be determined mainly through a national pay scale. If the autonomy that providers experience is to be meaningful, however, than it is probable that providers should be allowed some flexibility over financial matters. An important component of this is likely to be flexibility over pay and conditions. This provides managers with the capacity to be responsive to local conditions and challenges. Flexibility over pay may help employers address shortages they face in particular areas by offering higher wages for these positions or raise wages to take account of high housing costs that might deter people from applying to the hospital.

Although financial flexibility is likely to be important for local autonomy, and is useful for developing a responsive service, it is also associated with a number of potential pitfalls. Although these features do not necessarily undermine the case for flexibility, they nevertheless highlight that these financial freedoms impose costs as well as benefits. One issue relates to the conditions of new joiners to a workforce. One worry is that while the employment conditions of those who are transferred out of a state-run health service to a foundation hospital may be protected, these guarantees may not be extended to new joiners to the hospital workforce. These entrants are likely to join on terms inferior to existing members of staff, thereby resulting in a two-tier workforce (Unison 2004). Steps might be taken to alleviate this problem. A minimum level of employment conditions, such as a minimum wage and pension rights, could be made part of the central standards that public services have to satisfy. Paul Maltby and Tim Gosling (2003) argue that a government insisting that any new joiners should not enjoy employment conditions that are less favourable than those of existing staff could adopt a 'no less favourable' clause. Of course, the content of this clause is likely to be the subject of intense debate, but the sort of things it may cover include sick pay, holiday entitlement and pension rights.

Context

As well as contemplating the internal constitution of foundation hospitals, it is also important to consider the environment in which they operate. Foundation hospitals can be implemented in a range of different environments. On one approach, foundation hospitals can be implemented in a way that does not allow users to exercise a choice between different hospitals. On this model, hospitals would be charged with serving a particular neighbourhood or district. Residents of this locality would only be allowed to attend their local hospital. Any user involvement would come in the form of voice. An alternative approach is to allow users to exercise choice as well as voice. Patients would be allowed to choose between different hospitals and individuals might be provided with financial support that would allow them to attend a range of hospitals. Attempts might also be made to enhance choice by arranging hospitals so that they have overlapping jurisdictions. This means that two or more hospitals could be required to make services available to the same region. Residents would have a choice of providers. This alternative approach resonates more strongly with the arguments of this book, which seeks to allow a role for both voice and choice.

Conclusion

This chapter has looked at issues surrounding the public interest company. This examination has been undertaken because the public interest company is an exemplar of the approach to public services set out in this book. I have sought to highlight the main features of the public interest company, and defended it against the charge that these organisations would be unworkable. To throw the spotlight on what this general model may mean in practice, I have looked at how this model might be applied to health. As the criticisms levelled at both the public interest company and foundation hospitals make clear, not all commentators are happy with these bodies. Having responded to these concerns, I now turn in the next chapter to more general criticisms of the policy stance set out in this book.

6 Criticisms and Concerns

Introduction

The previous chapters have forwarded a model of public services in which users have an active role in shaping the services they experience. User involvement through voice and choice is coupled with freedoms for providers within a framework of centrally defined standards. All of this adds up to a diverse model of public services with a range of providers. The shape of public services set out here is likely to stimulate controversy and opposition. In this chapter, I aim to address two prominent concerns with the approach mapped out in this book. The first are worries about equality. Equality is a key commitment of public services. Within public services, equality is often understood to imply equal access for those in equal need. This means that a person's need rather than their background should condition the level of service that they receive (Dixon et al. 2003; Organization for Economic Co-operation and Development 2004b). One concern with a plural model of public services relates to the threat it supposedly poses to equality. For example, David Walker (2002) argues that, in a society in which significant inequalities exist in the distribution of resources and opportunities, equality demands redistribution from the better off to the worse off. Walker argues that only the centre is capable of co-ordinating the necessary redistribution of resources. He contends that by moving away from the centre, a policy of encouraging a range of providers within public services threatens the pursuit of equality. Safeguarding equality requires centralisation. This worry about equality forms part of a wider concern about the capacity of decentralised systems to deliver a co-ordinated level of service. B. Guy Peters writes

decentralised form of governing is generally not capable of providing coherent and co-ordinated governance, and likewise is not good at deciding on broad priorities for the society. These requirements for effective governance are by no means guaranteed by the recentring of the state, but these changes may assist in rebuilding that capacity (Guy Peters 2004, 139).

Second are deeper worries about choice. The introduction of choice within public services is a controversial matter (Ladd 2002; Crouch 2003; Blomqvist 2004). Opposition to choice is not confined to those who favour centralised public services. Concerns also surface among those who are otherwise disposed to move beyond a centrally driven model of public services. These worries about choice transfer straightforwardly to the version of public services set out in this book. In this chapter, I try to address both of these concerns. Although I concede that many of the above critics may be unconvinced by the arguments put forward in this chapter, I hope to persuade other readers that the approach adopted in this book may go some way in accommodating the above concerns. The first part of the chapter considers issues surrounding equality. The second part of the chapter examines criticisms of using choice within public services.

Equality and difference

Allowing a diverse range of providers into public services is likely to lead to differences in outcome within public services. For example, it is probable that different providers will respond in different ways to the varying demands of their users and employees. Acknowledging such differences does not necessarily mean that a plural version of public services is inimical to equality. While equality requires that differences in access between those in equal need be overcome, it does not necessarily call for the removal of all differences (Tawney 1931; Walzer 1983; Callinicos 2000). R.H. Tawney notes

> equality of provision is not identity of provision. It is to be achieved not by treating different needs in the same way, but by devoting equal care to ensuring that they are met in the different ways most appropriate to them, as is done by a doctor who prescribes different regimens for different constitutions, or a teacher who develops different types of intelligence by different curricula (Tawney 1931, 50–51).

Tawney argues that equality demands that equal consideration is provided to all individuals. Different people are subject, however, to different circumstances and possess differing endowments. Tawney says that treating people equally means tailoring public intervention to different circumstances and endowments. This implies that public provision will not be the same for all. Instead public intervention will vary according to circumstances and endowments. Equality thus requires a diversity of provision.

The different circumstances that people inhabit provide a case for treating people differently. However, even if different people occupy the same position and are subject to the same circumstances, equality allows differences to emerge. In particular, differences rooted in the different choices of people are broadly legitimate. In a work context, if one person decides to forgo a bit of leisure in favour of work, and a different person in a similar set of circumstances chooses to do the reverse, then the differences in income that result between these two people can be regarded as fair (White 1997; Dworkin 2000; Dixon et al. 2003). Anna Dixon et al. (2003) argue that equality of access within public services only requires that individuals have the same opportunities to use the service. They say that if people are provided with opportunities but choose not to use them, then the resulting inequalities of utilisation ought not to be seen as inequitable.

Equality allows differences to occur, both because of the different circumstances that people experience as well as the different choices that they make. These points are relevant to the version of public services put forward in this book. As we have seen, the capability approach is sensitive to individual circumstances and conditions. It recognises that people may require a greater share of resources in order to be able to do or be various things. Treating people equally, that is allowing everyone to develop similar capacities, does not require identity of provision. Furthermore, the emphasis placed on expanding the choices people can make within public services allows differences to emerge in relation to choice. The differences that are likely to be linked to the view of public services in this book should not be automatically regarded as inequitable. However, recognising this point still leaves open the issue of whether a centralised or decentralised system is better placed at tackling those inequalities that are regarded as unjust. Commentators who express reservations about the impact that a plural model of public services has on equality usually emphasise the importance of achieving equality through redistribution. This makes a connection between centralisation and equality. Centralisation is not the only route, however, for achieving equality. Equality might also be achieved through empowerment. This provides a connection between decentralisation and equality. For instance, Paul Hirst (1996) advocates 'associative democracy' as a way of promoting equality. Associative democracy implies that voluntary self-governing associations are the prime means of governance of economic and social affairs. A principle of subsidiarity is applied which means that power is distributed to the lowest level that is consistent with the execution of these affairs. Associative democracy concentrates on stressing the active participation of users within public services. Hirst suggests that by emphasising a combination of voice and exit, pressure will be placed on public service providers to take steps to enhance equality (Hirst 1996). Redistribution and empowerment constitute different ways of tackling inequality. Of course, these strategies are not mutually exclusive. For instance, it is possible to rely on the centre to redistribute income and assets through the tax and benefit system, while relying on voice or choice as a strategy for empowerment in the system of provision. Different systems offer different ways of promoting equality of access. The issue of which particular system is best placed to tackle inequality is in large part an empirical question. Faced with competing theoretical arguments about the advantages and disadvantages of different systems, evidence is important for assessing the merits of different systems. With this in mind, it is important to turn to evidence that compares different systems.

Evidence

A number of recent studies shed some light on the capacity of different types of systems to secure equality. Much of the available evidence comes from projects looking at the impact of different systems in guaranteeing equality within health. Two recent studies have focused on inequalities in countries within the Organization for Economic Co-operation and Development. Eddy van Doorslaer et al. (2002) examine health inequalities in the following 14 countries within the OECD: United States, Canada, Austria, Belgium, Denmark, Germany, Greece, Ireland, Italy, Luxembourg, Netherlands, Portugal, Spain and the United Kingdom. They use data collected in the 1996 wave of surveys carried out in the different countries. In the United States, data is taken from the Medical Expenditure Panel Survey, in Canada, data is provided by the National Population Health Survey and in the case of European countries the European Community Household Panel provides material. Van Doorslaer, Koolman and Puffer study differences in the use of physicians by people from different income groups within the different countries. In common with many other researchers, van Doorslaer, Koolman and Puffer use inequalities in use as a proxy for inequalities in access. Anna Dixon et al. (2003) say that it is preferable when studying access to look at the opportunities available to individuals because this takes into account whether or not people choose to use a service. However, difficulties in ascertaining whether the different uses of service are rooted in the different choices that people make means that empirical research into access tends to focus on use.

Need is an important factor determining the use of physicians. The greater a person's need, the more likely they are to approach and use a physician. To help isolate the impact of income, these researchers present results that take account of need. They examine differences in use among people from different income groups with the same level of need. Van Doorslaer, Koolman and Puffer report that visits to physicians in the countries surveyed are connected fairly to need and not income. They note that the only exceptions to this pattern emerge in Greece, Austria, United States and Portugal, where a significant bias towards the rich is observed (with Portugal having the largest pro-rich bias). Van Doorslaer, Koolman and Puffer then go on to break down the general category of physicians into visits to general practitioners and visits to medical specialists. Survey data allows them to do this in all countries except the United States. These researchers find that the results for physicians are the net effect for different trends for general practitioners and medical specialists. They say that there is a pro-poor bias in a majority of the European countries and Canada for visits to general practitioners. Portugal and Austria possess a pro-rich bias. Van Doorslaer, Koolman and Puffer go on to mention that only Spain, Ireland, Luxembourg and Belgium have a statistically significant (i.e. the results are statistically robust) pro-poor bias. In terms of visits to medical specialists, these researchers note that with the exception of Luxembourg there exists a bias towards the rich in all the European countries and Canada. The results for the pro-rich bias are all statistically significant. These academics write that, 'Overall, in all countries except the United States, Portugal, Greece and Austria, *total* doctor visits appear to be distributed according to need, although the *type* of doctor seen varies with income' (Van Doorslaer et al. 2002, 241). They say that the fact that this finding emerges within countries with different types of health care systems suggest that inequalities may be due more to differences in behaviour of lower and higher income individuals rather than differences in health systems.

Eddy van Doorslaer and Cristina Masseria (2004) update and extend the above analysis in their study of health inequalities in the following 21 OECD countries: Australia, Austria, Belgium, Canada, Denmark, Finland, France, Germany, Greece, Hungary, Ireland, Italy, Mexico, Netherlands, Norway, Portugal, Spain, Sweden, Switzerland, United Kingdom and United States. Van Doorslaer and Masseria concentrate mainly on data contained within the 2001 wave of national surveys. As before, van Doorslaer and Masseria study differences in the use of physicians by different income groups. However, this time, physicians are broken down into three groups: general practitioners, medical specialists and dentists. They report a slight pro-poor bias in the number of visits to general practitioners across different countries. Statistically significant pro-poor biases are found in Belgium, Canada, Denmark, Finland, Greece, Ireland, Italy, Netherlands, Spain and the United Kingdom. Van Doorslaer and Masseria continue that there is little inequity in the probability of seeing a general practitioner across most OECD countries. In relation to medical specialists, there is a pro-rich bias in the number of visits to specialists and probability of seeing a medical specialist in all countries. The Netherlands has the lowest statistically significant pro-rich bias on the number and probability of visits to medical specialists. All countries report a pro-rich bias for the number and probability of visits to dentists, and with the exception of the statistics for the number of dental visits in Belgium, all these results are statistically significant.

The findings in the above studies conducted under the auspices of the OECD are echoed in one of the surveys conducted by the School of Public Health at Harvard and the Commonwealth Fund of New York. Robert Blendon, Cathy Schoen, Catherine DesRoches, Robin Osborn, Kimberley Scholes and Kinga Zapert (2002) look at inequalities in access within Australia, Canada, New Zealand, United Kingdom and United States. The results are derived from telephone interviews conducted with a representative sample of the adult population conducted in each country between April and May 2001. Around 1400 individuals were interviewed in each country. Respondents were classified as lower or higher income depending on whether they fell below or above the median income within each country. As part of the survey, individuals were asked about access to medical services. Although a majority of higher income and lower income people did not say that access to health had worsened over the past two years, lower income people were more likely to say that access to health services had worsened over the past two years. For lower income people, the figures ranged from around 20 per cent of respondents (Australia and United Kingdom) to 28 per cent (Canada). For higher income people, the figures went from 12 per cent (New Zealand) to 24 per cent (Canada). The researchers say that with the exception of Canada, differences between income groups were statistically significant. They say that lower income people also report greater difficulty in having access to specialist care. The proportion of lower income individuals who stated that they found it very or extremely difficult to see a specialist ranged from 14 per cent in Australia to 30 per cent in the United States. The corresponding figures for higher income individuals went from 6 per cent in New Zealand to 14 per cent in Canada. The researchers say that the income disparities were statistically significant for all countries except Australia.

At least two conclusions can be discerned from the above studies. All the systems surveyed are characterised by some form of inequality. Inequality is a feature of both centralised and decentralised systems. Inequality is a feature of a relatively centralised system such as Britain as well as more decentralised systems such as France or Switzerland. The existence of inequality across the different systems examined suggests that inequality is a challenge for all systems. Second, while inequality is a policy concern whatever systems one favours, it is difficult to say that one system is unequivocally better than others. A centralised system such as Britain fares better than some more decentralised systems in some regards, but also worse in others. It is difficult to point to a clear advantage of centralisation over decentralisation or vice versa, for the pursuit of equality.

Centralisation and inequality

The view that centralisation is associated with important inequalities receives confirmation from studies looking at the record of centralisation in eradicating inequality. Britain has one of the most centralised health systems in the world (Blank and Burau 2004). A recent review of inequality within the NHS in Britain indicates that inequality has existed for some time (Dixon et al. 2003). In their review of the empirical evidence, Anna Dixon et al. (2003) make a distinction between 'macro' and 'micro' studies. Macro-studies look at the use of most or all health services by specific groups and compare this with the needs of groups indicated by general measures of self-reporting. Micro-studies examine utilisation of particular services or treatment procedures, usually using clinical records rather than self-reporting to establish need. Dixon, Le Grand, Henderson, Murray and Poteliakhoff argue that the macro- and micro-studies provide different pictures of the pattern on inequality. In terms of the macro-evidence, they say that early studies suggest that utilisation of the NHS favoured the better off. Dixon, Le Grand, Henderson, Murray and Poteliakhoff note that these early studies were conducted in the late 1970s and early 1980s, often based on data received from General Household Survey, an annual survey of 33,000 people in Great Britain (Forster 1976; Le Grand 1978). Dixon et al. continue that studies conducted during the late 1980s pointed to a more equal pattern (O'Donnell et al. 1991; Evandrou et al. 1992), while the most comprehensive recent study, based on data from the annual Health Survey in England supports findings from the earlier studies (Sutton et al. 2002).

In contrast to the macro-studies, they say that a review of micro-studies reveals that there is strong evidence that lower socio-economic groups use services less in relation to need than those from higher socio-economic groups. For example, they say that studies have found that coverage of screening for cancer care is poorer for lower socio-economic groups (Gatrell et al. 1998); the level of cardiac care (such as admissions and rate of investigation) tend to favour the better off (Goddard and Smith 2001); there exist lower rates of elective surgery (for things such as hernia) for lower socio-economic groups in relation to need (Seymour and Garthwaite 1999); inequalities in provision for chronic disease, for instance, with poorer provision of diabetes clinics and reviews in deprived areas (Khunti 2001) and lower levels of continuity of care for antenatal, labour and postnatal community care for those mothers from lower socio-economic groups (Hemingway et al. 1997).

These authors suggest that the discrepancies in the methodologies deployed in the macro- and micro-studies help explain the differences in the findings generated by these two broad types of study. For example, they argue that the different way that need is measured between macro- and micro-studies has an impact on the results. They continue that the more objective measures used in micro-studies (which uses clinical records rather than self-reporting) mean that micro-evidence tends to be of a higher quality and more reliable. They contend that micro-evidence provides strong evidence of the presence of inequalities.

Choice and equality

Concerns about equality are not restricted to possible impact that a decentralised system of public services has on equality. Worries are also expressed over one of the techniques set out in this book, namely the role allowed for choice. This line of criticism does not focus on differences between broad systems – that is a centralised and decentralised model of public services – but rather on the character of a plural system. One of the areas that these worries often surface is in relation to school choice. For example, Terry Moe comments that within debates in the United States a, 'common argument against school choice is that it leads to equity problems' (Moe 2002, 179). A range of individuals express criticisms about the impact of choice on equality (Wells 1993; Fuller 1996; Fiske and Ladd 2000, 2001). We have come into contact with some of these concerns in Chapter 4 during the discussion of cream-skimming. The worry here is that cream-skimming will undermine equality of access for those in equal need by serving to exclude people from poor or minority backgrounds. An assessment of the link between choice and equality ought to start by acknowledging the choices that already exist in most systems of public service provision (Hill and Guin 2002). In a system in which parents are not formally allowed to choose between different schools and children attend the school in their neighbourhood, richer individuals can choose between schools by being able to move houses near good schools. Houses near good schools command a premium that only the rich are able to afford. Alternatively, rich people can avoid sending their children to a local under-performing school by opting out of the state system and paying for private schooling. Paul Hill and Kacey Guin (2002) characterise these choices as covert choices. They say that, 'What matters is whether everyone or just some people have choices, and whether choices are made openly or in secret' (Hill and Guin 2002, 19). The issue then is not whether or not there should be choice, but rather whether the choices available to the few should be made more generally available. A number of reviews of choice suggest that much depends on how it is shaped and implemented. However, these reviews conclude that if implemented carefully, choice can yield benefits in terms of equality (Hill 2002; Working Commission on Choice in K-12 Education 2004; Burgess et al. 2005). Ted Fiske and Helen Ladd (2000, 2001) highlight the harm that choice may do to equality in their analysis of the introduction of school choice within New Zealand. In 1991, a reform was introduced into schools in New Zealand that allowed parents to choose schools. Once schools hit full capacity, however, schools were allowed to select pupils. Fiske and Ladd report that this policy led to an increase in segregation by ethnicity and socio-economic background. Other scholars have questioned parts of this analysis (Hill 2002; Burgess et al. 2005). Simon Burgess et al. (2005) argue that the main problem with the New Zealand reforms were that it introduced choice on the demand side without taking steps also to open up the supply side.

Caroline Hoxby (2003a, b) provides a more positive analysis of the effects of choice. Hoxby examines the impact of school choice in Milwaukee (in Wisconsin), Michigan and Arizona. She examines the use of vouchers within Milwaukee (noted in Chapter 1). In Michigan and Arizona, Hoxby looks at the impact of charter schools. These are schools chartered by the government in response for a fee. Voucher-accepting schools are usu-ally required to accept a voucher applicant through a lottery, although they may also practice selective admission. Charter schools are required to use a lottery or accept pupils on the basis of 'negative' criteria (for instance, if a student indicates that he or she would like to drop out of school). Overall, Hoxby finds that these choice schemes help improve productivity (defined as improvements in pupil achievement per dollar that is spent) throughout the schools system. She says that improvements are not confined to those schools accepting vouchers or are charter institutions. Instead, school choice is a 'rising tide that floats all boats'. Moreover, she argues that evidence suggests that voucher-accepting schools and charter schools do not cream-skim along racial, ethnic or social grounds. Indeed, the evidence suggests that bodies such as charter schools disproportionately attract students who were subject to discrimination elsewhere in the system of public schools. Caroline Hoxby's analysis has not been uncontested. Helen Ladd argues that Hoxby's analysis of the Milwaukee programme is problematic because Hoxby is unable to control properly for the changing mix of students in her treatment and control groups. Ladd says that the inability to track adequately the same individuals over time reduces the robustness of her results (Ladd 2002). While the size of the improvements is the subject of debate, Hoxby does provide evidence of the way that choice may help bolster performance.

Choice

The above evidence suggests that if used carefully choice can enhance equality. However, much depends on how it is shaped and implemented. Worries about choice go deeper though than a concern with equality. A broader set of reservations see choice as a threat to citizenship (Crouch 2003; Needham 2003; Marquand 2004). This critique draws a distinction between citizens and consumers. Choice tends to be associated with a consumer model of society. On this view, emphasising choice is to treat people as consumers. Critics allege that the problem with this is that while consumerism is appropriate to the sphere of the market, it is not suitable for the public domain. Consumerism is alien to the assumptions and principles of public services and citizenship. Introducing choice within the public domain will simply hollow out citizenship. David Marquand comments that the, 'language of buyer and seller, producer and consumer, does not belong in the public domain; nor do the relationships which this language implies. People are consumers only in the market domain; in the public domain, they are citizens' (Marquand 2004, 135). These reservations about choice do not mean that critics support a centralised model of public services. Colin Crouch and David Marquand both favour a more active role for individuals within public services, but wish this to be conducted on the basis of voice not choice.

Various commentators suggest that choice forms part of a broader attempt to commercialise public services. For instance, Colin Crouch (2003) contends that commercialisation represents the replacement of the assumptions and principles of the public realm with those of the private sector. He says that commercialisation undermines citizenship in two main ways. First, commercialisation distorts in a negative fashion the character of the goods provided to citizens. He states that providing 'goods or services through markets involves an elaborate procedure of creating barriers to access so that we cannot get them without payment. Sometimes the character of the good itself has to be changed to do this' (Crouch 2003, 9). Second, commercialisation threatens the universal availability of the goods provided to citizens. He argues that commercial bodies only target those sections that are good for business. The result is the provision of a residual rather than universal service to individuals. Citizenship, in contrast, is committed to universal rights.

A different set of concerns takes issue with the willingness or capacity of people to exercise choice. Fiona Millar (2004) casts doubt on the notion that parents want to be able to exercise choice between schools. She says that parents simply want to have a good local school. Barry Schwartz (2004) questions whether expanding choice is always a good thing, saying that there is a wealth of psychological evidence that it can in fact bring people misery and unhappiness. Among other things, people can become unhappy about the foregone opportunities that are implied when they make a particular choice and feel bewildered by the choices that are made available. Furthermore, John Clarke and Elizabeth Vidler (2004) contend that not everybody will be equally good at exercising choice. They suggest that people draw upon a variety of personal resources to exercise choice. They highlight the role of 'cultural' or 'symbolic' forms of capital, which covers things such as how articulate people are. An unequal distribution of these forms of capital means that choice will favour the most articulate members of society.

Citizens or consumers?

The idea that people are either citizens or consumers implies a strict separation of these models of human behaviour. It suggests that each model possesses their own unique assumptions and principles. As individual choice belongs to the realm of consumerism, it is a mistake to try to introduce this within the world of citizenship. Such a dichotomy fails to recognise, however, that while consumerism and citizenship are plausibly different models of human activity, they have elements in common. While certain features may be specific to either consumerism or citizenship, there are other components that exist in both fields. Choice is arguably one such element. Although choice is shaped in different ways within citizenship and consumerism, it is a common element of both these models of human behaviour. It is true that choice has been most closely associated with consumerism in recent times. However, a refusal to engage with choice because of this association simply allows choice to be defined by those in favour of consumerism. Choice is arguably too important to be left to develop in this fashion.

Within citizenship, the right to choose is an important component of individual autonomy (Beauchamp and Childress 2001; Coulter 2002; Le Grand 2003a). Tom Beauchamp and James Childress (2001) argue that autonomy is a basic principle of morality. They argue that the right to choose is central to the concept of autonomy. They comment that to, 'respect an autonomous agent is, at a minimum, to acknowledge that person's right to hold views, to make choices, and to take actions based on personal values and beliefs' (Beauchamp and Childress 2001, 63). Beauchamp and Childress contend that several conditions are needed for autonomous actions. First, individuals should take intentional actions. They say that this is not a matter of degree as actions are either intentional or unintentional. Second, the actions should be undertaken with understanding. Beauchamp and Childress state that understanding is a matter of degree, as actions are capable of being taken with greater or lesser degrees of understanding. Third, actions should be independent of controlling influences. Beauchamp and Childress say that this is also a matter of degree, as individuals are subject to varying degrees of outside influence. They continue that autonomy does not require that people should have the fullest possible understanding or the least possible existence of outside interference. Rather, autonomy only requires that people have a substantial degree of understanding or lack of outside influence. They say that to,

> restrict adequate decision-making by patients and research subjects to the
> ideal of fully or completely autonomous decision-making strips their acts
> of any meaningful place in the practical world, where people's actions are
> rarely, if ever, fully autonomous. A person's appreciation of information
> and independence from controlling influences in the context of health

care need not exceed, for example, a person's information and independence in making a financial investment, hiring a new employee, buying a house, or selecting a university (Beauchamp and Childress 2001, 59–60).

Beauchamp and Childress say that respecting a person's autonomy in healthcare implies supporting a person's right to choose and play an active role within decision-making as regards health. Individuals should be able to exercise choice over the course of treatment that they undertake. To support the autonomous choices of patients, healthcare professionals need to disclose relevant information to patients. Doctors can aid understanding by answering patient queries or drawing analogies between medical information and issues more familiar to patients. Beauchamp and Childress note that the right to choose covers the right of patients to delegate decision-making to health professionals.

The idea of a right to choose is not new to the concept of citizenship. People have long experienced a right to choose with the civil and political aspects of citizenship. In relation to civil rights, choice is a dimension of freedom of expression. People are broadly free to express whatever opinions they choose provided this does not harm other citizens. With respect to political citizenship, choice is intrinsic to the right to vote. Part of the story of how citizenship developed concerns how the choices available to some were made available to others. The early part of the twentieth century, for example, saw efforts to provide women with the same voting rights as men. The issue is not whether is choice alien to the traditions of citizenship but rather whether the choice that exists within civil and political citizenship should be extended more comprehensively within social rights.

Evidence exists that suggests that there is support among the public within different countries for exercising choice within public services. Within the United States, Jeanne Lambrew (2005) reports on data on choice from a biennial health insurance survey conducted on behalf of the health policy institute, the Commonwealth Fund of New York. The survey was conducted from September 2003 to January 2004 and a nationally representative sample of adults aged 19 or over were interviewed by telephone, focusing in particular on 3293 adults belonging to the working age (19–64) population. Part of the survey looked at the attitudes of respondents to having a choice between different providers, as well as having choice over various health plans offered to them. Lambrew notes that members of the working age population with employer sponsored insurance who do not have a choice over where medical attention is received are more dissatisfied than those who do have such a choice. Twenty-six per cent of those with no choice of provider were somewhat or very dissatisfied with healthcare as opposed to 4 per cent of those who did have such a choice. Also, those who did not have a choice of health plan were slightly more dissatisfied (12 per cent) than those who did have a plan (10 per cent). The survey also indicated that choice was popular across different income groups. Fifty-seven per cent of those earning less than $20,000 per year thought it very important that employers offer more than one health plan, and these sentiments were shared by 60 per cent of those earning between $20,000 and $34,999, 57 per cent of those earning between $35,000 and $59,999 and 58 per cent of those earning more than $60,000. Those who thought that choice of health plan was not too important range from 11 per cent of those earning less than $20,000, 14 per cent of those earning between $20,000 and $34,999, 16 per cent of those earning between $35,000 and $59,999 and 17 per cent of those earning more than $60,000. Individuals were also generally confident about their capacity to exercise choice. A total of 73 per cent of those earning less than $20,000 felt very or somewhat confident in choosing a health plan without employer help. The figures for those earning between $20,000 and $34,999, $35,000 and $59,999 and more than $60,000 were 73 per cent, 72 per cent and 77 per cent, respectively.

A different study echoes the above findings. The Employee Benefit Research Institute based in Washington DC has an annual series of health confidence surveys looking at the attitudes of the American public towards health policy in the United States. As part of a survey conducted between 18 April and 19 May 2002, questions were asked about choice. Telephone interviews were conducted with a sample of 1000 people aged 21 or over. Respondents were asked questions about the ability to choose among hospitals, doctors and prescription drugs. The survey found that majorities favoured the exercise of choice. For example, 81 per cent of respondents cited the ability to choose among doctors as extremely or very important, while 77 per cent of people thought the ability to choose among hospitals as very or extremely important and 79 per cent of individuals considered the ability to choose the insurance that cover the prescription drugs they take as very or extremely important (Employee Benefit Research Institute 2002).

Within Europe, Angela Coulter and Helen Magee (2004) report on a project on choice conducted on behalf of the Picker Institute Europe. This project examined the attitudes of citizens in eight European countries towards their health care systems. The countries examined were as follows: Germany, Italy, Poland, Slovenia, Spain, Sweden, Switzerland and the United Kingdom. As part of this study, telephone surveys were carried out by NIPO (a Netherlands based market research institute) with around 1000

Table 1 *Want free choice of provider (by country)*

	Germany n = 1026 (%)	Italy n = 1021 (%)	Poland n = 1050 (%)	Slovenia n = 1014 (%)	Spain n = 1000 (%)	Sweden n = 1000 (%)	Switzerland n = 1000 (%)	United Kingdom n = 1008 (%)
Primary care doctors	98	86	98	98	89	86	93	87
Specialist doctors	97	83	95	87	86	31	84	79
Hospitals	94	85	94	86	78	54	85	80

Source: Angela Coulter and Helen Magee (eds) *The European Patient of the Future* (Maidenhead: Open University): 224; table 11.10. Reproduced with the kind permission of the Open University Press/McGraw-Hill Publishing Company.

individuals in each of these countries in July 2002. These interviews were conducted with a random sample of the adult population (defined as those who are over the age of 16). The telephone survey examined the public's attitudes towards having a choice of provider. People were asked about being allowed a choice between primary care doctors (that is general practitioners), specialist doctors and hospitals. Table 1 presents some of the results that were gained from this survey.

The research found that substantial majorities within the eight countries surveyed wanted to have a choice within primary care. The lowest majority of 86 per cent was found in Italy and Sweden. Large majorities were detected in seven countries for choice over specialist doctors, the exception being Sweden where a majority did not want this choice. Sweden was also an exception in relation to the issue of hospital choice, recording only a slight majority (54 per cent) in favour of this in comparison to considerable majorities elsewhere. The research found that choice was popular across all age groups, with the young being slightly more favourable to choice than older people. Choice was also popular across people with different educational backgrounds, with those who only had primary education more disposed to choice than those who had secondary or higher education. Overall, the results indicate that there is strong support for choice from the citizens who were surveyed.

I have suggested above that choice is not alien to the concept of citizenship and that there is evidence that a substantial proportion of the public in different countries are willing to exercise choice in areas such as health. A separate issue relates to the different capacities of people to exercise choice (Beauchamp and Childress 2001; Clarke and Vidler 2004). As mentioned above, John Clarke and Elizabeth Vidler (2004) worry that the implementation of choice will favour those who are best able to conduct choice. This concern about choice extends to all forms of citizenship participation. Some people are likely to be better able at expressing voice than others, for the same sorts of reasons that Clarke and Vidler discuss in relation to choice. Helen Richards, et al. (2002) provide some evidence of the link between voice and inequality in their study of differences in perceptions and responses to chest pain among people in different income groups in Glasgow, Scotland. Richards, Reid and Watt note that a recent 21-country study into coronary heart disease reported that Glasgow had the highest mortality rate from coronary heart disease among all the locations studied. Richards, Reid and Watt sought to explore how differences in socio-economic background impacted on the take-up of cardiac services. They conducted a qualitative study, interviewing 30 adults in a deprived area of Glasgow and 30 adults in an affluent part of the city. The respondents were aged 45–64 years old. Richards, Reid and Watt found that those in deprived areas reported a greater perceived vulnerability to heart disease, as a result of a family history of the disease as well as the lifestyles they led. The academics found that this greater perceived vulnerability did not, however, translate into greater reporting to a general practitioner. Richards, Reid and Watt note that the quality of interactions with general practitioner mould people's responses to perceived illness. Interaction covers things such as the extent to which people feel they belong to the same social level as their doctor, the extent to which information is shared between doctor and patient and the degree to which people blame themselves for their perceived illness. The researchers discovered that those living in more affluent areas had greater social connections with health professionals, reported a greater sharing of knowledge with their doctor and blamed themselves less than those in deprived areas. The researchers suggest that the better quality of interaction that the more affluent appeared to enjoy with their doctors may help explain the different rates of take-up of cardiac services by people from different socio-economic backgrounds.

It is an open question whether choice or voice suffers from greater problems in this regard. However, in response to the specific concern about choice (which by extension also applies to voice), it is likely that people will possess different capacities to exercise choice. Indeed, I have suggested that one of the attractions of the capability approach is that it allows those individuals who require a greater share of resources than others in order to develop a given level of being or doing to have access to such resources. Although the capability approach can take steps to address the concern about the capacity to exercise choice, for example by providing additional education or information for those who require greater support to make informed choices, it is probable that some differences will remain. These differences can be a source of inequality between persons.

One response to the continued existence of differences is to reject all attempts to foster choice. However, this solution raises issues of its own. Not allowing choices to be made by users means that decisions will be taken by either government officials, public servants or both. We have already seen that one of the challenges that public services face is adapting to the expectations of the public. It is unclear that a policy of relying on government officials or public servants will be sufficient to meet this task, particularly when existing forms of limited user involvement have not quelled all expectations. Furthermore, placing all decision-making into the hands of government officials or public servants puts them in a position of power over users. This position of power raises a problem because it endangers the autonomy experienced by users. The importance of enhancing the autonomy of users casts doubt on the desirability of leaving all decision-making in the hands of bureaucrats or public servants. Thus, while the problems posed by the different capacities to exercise choice should be acknowledged, and steps taken to reduce such differences as far as possible, the existence of different capacities does not destroy the case for choice. The alternative of avoiding choice altogether creates difficulties of its own.

If we accept the above argument, then the issue is not whether public policy ought to broaden the choices available to users, but rather what should be the extent of the available choices. Although the evidence that Barry Schwartz provides cautions against too much choice, it does not support the view that there should be no choice at all. Schwartz does not deny the importance of choice, only the value of too much choice. He states that, 'having the opportunity to choose is essential to well-being, but choice has negative features, and the negative features escalate as the number of choices increases' (Schwartz 2004, 222). The issue then is how constrained choice ought to be, not that there should be moves to drive out choice completely. Of course, deciding how constrained choice ought to be is not an easy matter. However, the answer to this (which is likely to be manifold in nature, with different levels of choice appropriate for different public services), can only be discerned by engaging rather than rejecting the agenda on choice.

Conclusion

This chapter has considered two prime concerns with the version of public services set out in this book. First, I have looked at concerns that moving away from a centralised view of public services will undermine the quest for equality. Second, I have addressed worries that the introduction of choice will threaten citizenship. In relation to equality, I have acknowledged that a plural model of public services is likely to lead to differences within public service. However, the presence of these differences does not necessarily undermine equality because equality is compatible with some differences, both because of the individual choices that people make and because of tailoring policy to the different circumstances that people experience. Evidence of equality from international studies suggests that both centralised and decentralised systems face challenges in tackling inequality, and it is not obvious that one system is clearly superior to another. As regards concerns that choice may worsen inequality, evidence suggests that a lot depends on how choice is shaped and put into place. Choice has the potential to improve performance and bolster equality.

With respect to choice and citizenship, choice can be defended as a part of citizenship. Choice is an important element of individual autonomy, and choice is already exercised in the civil and political aspects of citizenship. Evidence suggests that there is support among the public for extending choice within the social realm of citizenship. The differences that exist between the capacities of different people to exercise choice does not automatically undermine a case for choice as the alternative of preventing the choices of citizens raises difficulties of its own.

Conclusion

Public services today have to confront a series of important challenges. Although some of the challenges that services in different countries face are a product of the particular institutions, historical background and interactions between competing interests within that country, there are also issues that cut across national boundaries. These challenges are both intellectual and practical in orientation. Chapter 1 mentioned four of these challenges. These relate to the dissatisfaction that users feel about the services they experience, rising costs of providing services caused by demographic changes and the pace of technological development, intellectual criticisms of public services from the 'New Right' spectrum of political opinion and changes within the global economy and society. Of course, one can overstate these cross-cutting issues. For instance, in relation to people's expectations or perceptions of public services, surveys often reveal that people are more pessimistic about the state of public services as a whole than over their own local services. Thus, people may be more satisfied with their local school or hospital than with the health or education system as a whole. This raises the possibility that, fuelled perhaps by media scare stories, people have an unfairly jaundiced view of public services as a whole. Similarly, the notion that globalisation is overturning all economic and social structures in its path does not stand up to close scrutiny. Although one should not exaggerate the issues faced, it is nevertheless the case that public services face a series of serious challenges. Even if people have an overly pessimistic view of public services as a whole, this matters if it helps erode public support for the collective funding of these services. If people do not think that their taxes are being well spent, they might put pressure on politicians to cut taxes at a time when the costs of services are rising. Likewise, the idea that globalisation is not tearing up the economic and social fabric of most countries does not mean that it has not helped create problems through the impetus it provides for pluralism, the health risks that cut across national boundaries and the fillip it has given to the consumer society.

For much of the twentieth century, public services have been viewed through the prisms of the centralised state or free market. Of course, as has been noted in Chapter 1, the fields of comparative political economy and governance have pointed out that the reality of public services was often

127

more complex than a model in which the central state has a monopoly over the funding and provision of public services or a situation in which people's need for health and education services is delivering through profit-seeking firms competing in the marketplace. This has fed intellectual currents that explore the terrain beyond the state and free market. While the state versus market approach provides a flawed description of reality, it continued to shape many policy discussions and ideas. The spread of free market ideas testifies to the significance of the market perspective. At the same time, the opposition that discussing moves away from the centralised state tends to generate indicates the emphasis still placed on central intervention in some quarters. One might try to accommodate the above challenges by resorting to either the state or free market. Such an approach, however, unnecessarily limits the options available to policy-makers. It closes off a range of avenues without proper investigation. The fact that state versus market thinking has not on the face of it prevented issues such as rising costs and public dissatisfaction presenting problems for public services suggests it may be worthwhile examining alternative policy directions.

A participative model of public services

I have sought to explore one particular way of organising public services. Put simply, I have examined the features of a participative model in which users of public services play a more active role within the services they experience. Citizenship provides the basic rationale for the provision of public services. Public services exist ultimately to support and sustain citizenship. Other notions such as fairness, oversight and accountability feed off our concept of citizenship. In line with the emphasis on citizenship, Chapter 2 put forward a view of citizenship based on the capacity of people to be able to be or do a range of things as well as the exercise of individual responsibility. This capability approach helps lay the foundation for an active or participative model of citizenship within public services. It points to providing people with resources so that they can play an active role in public services. While there is an obligation on the part of government to provide people with sufficient resources so that they can play an active role in public services, there is also a corresponding obligation on people to make proper use of these resources. It was suggested that individual activity within public services offers the potential for dealing with some of the problems that public services face. One way of tackling user dissatisfaction is to give them a greater role in the nature of the services they experience.

Capabilities are also sensitive to individual circumstances and so can adapt to the pluralism of circumstances and values inherent in modern society. Sensitivity to circumstances supports providing access to material resources and social rights. The criticisms directed at social citizenship were considered and rejected. Paying for services, however, is expensive and while the collective funding of services through taxation is an essential and core part of paying for services, rising costs means that there may have to be a role for user charges or systems of co-payment.

While capability and responsibility provide the basis for an active model of citizenship, participation can occur in different ways. People can either exercise a choice or voice within public services. Chapter 3 looked more closely at the question of the precise form that activity should take. I advanced a case for utilising both voice and choice. This was based on a critical engagement with arguably the most powerful New Right critique of the state, namely Friedrich Hayek's knowledge-based criticisms of central planning. Hayek argued that the presence of tacit or practical knowledge that is dispersed throughout a society creates an insuperable problem for a central agency wishing to co-ordinate plans. He says that competition allows this knowledge to be co-ordinated and so highlights a role for choice. While Hayek provides a case for choice, the generation of knowledge within a collective context opens up a role for voice within public services. In addition, the existence of coded or non-tacit forms of knowledge implies that a useful role can be played by central authorities.

Chapter 3 provided then a case for both voice and choice. This highlights that when thinking about the organisation of public services, one is not forced to go down a centralising route. Chapter 4 examined the sort of framework that is needed to support the exercise of choice and voice. It suggested a role for central authorities in helping to regulate choice and voice. Also, attention needs to be placed to ensuring there is enough capacity in the system of supply to allow people to express voice and choice. This emphasis on capacity allows a role for the private sector in providing spare capacity.

Chapter 5 continued the discussion of the supportive framework for user activity by looking more closely at what a commitment to central standards and local autonomy might mean in practical institutional terms. Attention was paid to the public interest company, as this exemplified the commitment to a notional public good as well as local autonomy. To illustrate some of the issues involved, I considered the sort of issues that need to be tackled when applying this model within health.

All of this implies a version of public services in which there is a range of providers. This model is likely to attract criticism, both because of concerns of the impact on equality as well as worries about a policy of introducing choice within public services. Chapter 6 considered these arguments, and while acknowledging that problems are likely to remain in a plural system of public services, as well as the fact as new problems are likely to emerge, there is at least a case for examining in more detail the potential offered by this alternative account.

Resistance

Some commentators may feel that the tone of my book is too Panglossian or optimistic, assuming that different techniques or institutions can be combined in an unproblematic fashion. Thus, choice can be easily combined with voice; the state, market and civil society can come together to fund and deliver public services and it is possible to blend together an attachment to the public interest with a corporate organisational form. A critic might argue that this ignores the fact that different institutions rest on different assumptions and foundations, and it is often not possible to combine these different institutions. Private sector bodies do not of necessity act in the public interest; the state and market are alternatives and not complements, with state spending for example crowding out private investment and choice will ultimately drive out voice. A sceptic may contend that a more realistic appraisal of the future of public services would recognise these conflicts and develop policy on the basis of such tensions.

Such a critique essentially returns one to the sort of states versus markets debates that this book is an attempt to escape from. I am alert to the tensions and difficulties that arise when trying to implement a diverse institutional mix. Institutions within different layers of a multi-level governance framework can be in conflict with one another. Tensions do occur between different nations and institutions of the European Union; an overbearing state can extinguish local autonomy and private and public sectors can exhibit mutual suspicion. While I do not wish to overlook such features, I do not think one should overstate them or use them to quash attempts to explore ways that public services might be organised in ways that differ from the dominant approaches after the end of the Second World War.

It is likely, however, that there will be resistance to the arguments presented in this book. In the preceding chapter we have seen some of the concerns of those who defend the state as well as more reform-minded progressives. In addition, trade unions have expressed worries about policies such as foundation hospitals. These worries will fuel resistance to moving towards the version of public services set out here. Overcoming such opposition is not an easy matter or is guaranteed. Two measures might be taken to address this opposition. The first would be to dispel some of the myths and misconceptions surrounding the sort of arguments advanced in this book. Painting measures such as foundation hospitals as an example of privatisation tends to cloud rather than clarify issues. It may well be that there are legitimate concerns about this policy measure. These will tend to be obscured, however, if this initiative is not properly understood. A first step to tackling resistance may be to clarify some of the issues involved. Second, there should be dispassionate and careful empirical analysis of the policies put forward in this book. Resistance can be attenuated by pointing to successful examples of the policies considered in this book. There is already evidence of these policies being adopted in different parts of the world. A challenge is to conduct a careful examination of such measures.

Future issues

Further research can be conducted on several fronts. First, further research can be conducted on the individual policy measures or initiatives that have been set out in this book. In my discussion of globalisation, I argue that an important role should be carved out for global institutions. The design of this global architecture is at an early stage of development, particularly when compared to the institutions that have arisen in national contexts. Global and transnational institutions, such as the United Nations, European Union, World Health Organization and World Trade Organization, exist and provide substance to the notion of a global civil society. However, the experience of such bodies suggest that the process of designing a robust set of institutions is not an easy matter, with concerns that organisations such as the European Union have a democratic deficit and forums such as the United Nations are dominated by the agendas of the richest and most powerful nations, and in particular the United States. The challenge is to develop bodies that command the support of political leaders in different countries, have sufficient legitimacy in the eyes of the public they serve and do not become a mouthpiece for dominant nations. Much remains to be done to tackling these issues and outlining the details of a robust set of transnational institutions.

Elsewhere I have suggested that the importance of fostering co-operation and organisational knowledge provides a case for implementing stakeholding. This stakeholding is manifested in bodies such as the public interest company.

Some observers suggest that while such organisations such as the public interest company are superficially attractive, it is important to work through a range of motivational issues before offering a full endorsement of such a policy (Le Grand 2003b). We have already seen that there may be difficulties in encouraging patients to vote in elections on foundation hospitals and so this raises the issue of how best to represent the interests of patients. It is useful to conduct a range of empirical studies on the public interest company to consider such issues. In areas such as transport, the environment and health, it is useful to study the motivations of different stakeholders and what information people require to play a full part in the governance of these organisations. More widely, it is valuable to focus on the tensions that arise between different stakeholders and what measures can be taken to ease these conflicts.

Second, it is worthwhile to examine further how different parts of a pluralist version of public services lock together. I have suggested that a multi-level governance approach is likely to be important for helping address globalisation and knowledge-based criticisms of central planning. One issue worth exploring is how these different layers of governance fit together. For instance, I argue that local autonomy should be set within a framework of national standards. However, in areas such as education, how should such standards be set? Who should be involved in the process of crafting these targets and what sources of information should be used to assess whether or not local bodies are meeting these standards? When conflicts arise between the centre and local bodies, how should they be negotiated and resolved?

One significant policy issue relates to how a pluralist model of public services can be implemented in practice. This book has concentrated on the way in which public services should be organised rather than developing a programme for reform. Furthermore, the principles discussed are of a general character rather than being fashioned for a specific national context. In moving, however, towards a pluralist version of public services, one has to take into account the constraints and opportunities imposed by different national contexts. Policy does not emerge from a blank slate but has to contend, among other things, with the legacies imposed by existing institutions, ideological traditions and domestic public opinion. The variety of different settings means that it is unlikely that the same transition path will be appropriate in all areas. Nor should we expect all countries to move towards exactly the same model of public services: different countries will negotiate the shape of a pluralist model of public services in different ways (some may give more weight to choice, others may have a different mix of public and private funding and so on). One interesting issue is to explore the path to reform in different countries and indeed within different sectors of the public services within the same country.

A third set of issues should study the overall impact of a pluralist model of public services. Will this help deliver a responsive set of institutions for a more demanding public? What is the impact on equality? Will this – as critics allege – worsen inequality or will this help erode the inequalities that already exist? All of the above map out a large programme of research. This befits the scale and importance of public services.

Notes

Introduction

1. Robert Blendon, Cathy Schoen, Catherine DesRoches, Robin Osborn, Kinga Zapert and Elizabeth Raleigh (2004) note that there are significant differences between the health systems of the United States, Canada, Australia, New Zealand and the United Kingdom. In the United States, hospitals operate within a decentralised and competitive insurance and delivery system. In Australia, public hospitals form the basis of hospital services. They compete with private providers in systems funded by universal public insurance that is supplemented by private insurance. In Canada and New Zealand, hospitals are run as public or 'not-for-profit' bodies, with budgets set annually by regional, provincial or district health authorities. In the United Kingdom, hospitals are run as public trusts which are funded mainly out of general taxation.

2. The Commission was chaired by Prof. Paul T. Hill, Director of the Center on Reinventing Public Education at the University of Washington at Seattle. The other commissioners were Prof. Julian Betts, Department of Economics, University of San Diego; David Ferrero, Director of Evaluation and Policy Research (Education) at The Bill & Melinda Gates Foundation; Brian P. Gill, Social Scientist, The RAND Corporation; Prof. Dan Goldhaber, Center on Reinventing Public Education, University of Washington; Laura Hamilton, Senior Behavioral Scientist, The RAND Corporation; Prof. Jeffrey R. Henig, Teachers College, Columbia University; Frederick M. Hess, Resident Scholar, The American Enterprise Institute; Tom Loveless, Director of Brown Center on Education Policy, the Brookings Institution; Prof. Stephen Macedo, Center for Human Values, Princeton University; Lawrence Rosenstock, Principal, High Tech High, San Diego; Charles Venegoni, Division Head, English and Fine Arts, John Hersey High School, Arlington Heights; Janet Weiss, Associate Provost for Academic Affairs, University of Michigan and Patrick J. Wolf, Asst Prof. of Public Policy, Georgetown University, Washington DC.

Problems of Central Planning

1. Choice in public services need not be confined to this type of choice. Adam Lent and Natalie Arend (2004) argue that people can also express choice within a particular provider, choosing among different options offered by a particular provider. They say choice-based lettings are an example of this. Here, a local authority offers its tenants a choice among a range of homes (such as number of rooms in a household, whether or not there is a garden, ground floor or first floor flat and so on). Lent and Arend continue that choice might also be exercised on a

collective basis, whereby people come together to make decisions about common public spaces, such as museums or parks.

Although choice can take different forms, my focus is on choice between providers. Collective versions of choice overlap importantly with the models of voice. This occurs particularly for those models of collective choice that arise from public deliberation. Analysing choice as an alternative to voice points to a scrutiny of choice between different providers or choice within providers. In discussions of choice of public services, choice between providers is the most common and controversial aspect of choice. Following this emphasis, I concentrate on this version of choice. In any case, many of the lessons that can be drawn from choice between providers can also be applied to choice within a provider.

References

6, P., Leat, D., Seltzer, K. and Stoker, G. (2002) *Towards Holistic Governance: The New Reform Agenda* (Basingstoke: Palgrave-Macmillan).

Ackerman, B. and Alstott, A. (1999) *The Stakeholder Society* (New Haven: Yale University Press).

Albert, M. (1993) *Capitalism against Capitalism* (London: Whurr Publishers).

Arnstein, S. (1969) 'A ladder of citizen participation', *Journal of the American Planning Association*, 35(4), 216–224.

Bache, I. and Flinders, M. (2004) *Multi-level Governance* (Oxford: Oxford University Press).

Barone, E. (1908) 'The Ministry of Production in the Collectivist State', reprinted in Hayek, F. (ed.)(1935) *Collectivist Economic Planning* (London: Routledge), 245–290.

Barr, N. (2001) *The Welfare State as Piggy Bank Information, Risk, Uncertainty and the Role of the State* (Oxford: Oxford University Press).

Beauchamp, T. and Childress, J. (2001) *Principles of Biomedical Ethics*, 5th edition (New York: Oxford University Press).

Bergson, A. (1948) 'Socialist Economies', in Ellis, H. (ed) *Survey of Contemporary Economies* (New York: Blakiston), 430–458.

Berlin, I. (1958) *Two Concepts of Liberty* (Oxford: Oxford University Press).

Besley, T. and Ghatak, M. (2003) 'Incentives, Choice and Accountability in the Provision of Public Services', *Oxford Review of Economic Policy,* 19(2), 235–249.

Birchall, J. (2002a) 'The implications for corporate governance of the proposed mutual ownership of water utilities and public transport', *Journal of Corporate Law Studies*, 2(1), 155–181.

Birchall, J. (2002b) *A Mutual Trend: How to Run Rail and Water in the Public Interest* (London: New Economics Foundation).

Birchall, J. and Simmons, R. (2002) *Final Report: A Theoretical Model of What Motivates Public Service Users to Participate* (Swindon: Economic and Social Research Council).

Blair, T. (1995) *Ownership and Control* (Washington, DC: The Brookings Institute).

Blair, T. (1998) *The Third Way: New Politics for a New Century* (London: The Fabian Society).

Blair, T. and Schroeder, G. (1999) 'Europe: the third way/die neue mitte', available at http://www.theamsterdampost.com/Archive/arc000006.html, accessed on 4 August 2005.

Blank, R. and Burau, V. (2004) *Comparative Health Policy* (Basingstoke: Palgrave).

Blendon, R.J. and DesRoches, C. (2003) 'Future healthcare challenges', *Issues in Science and Technology*, 19(4), 32–34.

Blendon, R.J., Schoen, C., DesRoches, C., Osborn, R. and Zapert, K. (2003) 'Common concerns amid diverse systems: health care experiences in five countries', *Health Affairs*, 22(3), 106–121.

Blendon, R, J., Schoen, C., DesRoches, C., Osborn, R., Scholes, K.L. and Zapert, K. (2002) 'Inequities in health care: a five country survey', *Health Affairs*, 21(1), 182–191.

Blendon, R.J., Schoen, C., DesRoches, C., Osborn, R., Zapert, K. and Raleigh, E. (2004) 'Confronting competing demands to improve quality: a five country hospital survey', *Health Affairs*, 23(3), 119–135.

Blomqvist, P. (2004) 'The choice revolution: privatization of Swedish welfare services in the 1990s', *Social Policy and Administration*, 38(2), 139–155.

Bowles, S. and Gintis, H. (1998) 'Efficient redistribution: new rules for markets, states and communities', in Wright, E.O. (ed.) *Recasting Egalitarianism: New Rules for Communities, States and Markets* (New York: Verso), 3–71.

Brecher, C. (2002) *The Public Interest Company as a Mechanism to Improve Service Delivery: Suggestions for the Reorganization of the London Underground and National Health Service Trusts* (London: Public Management Foundation).

Brewer, G.A. and Coleman Selden, S. (1998) 'Whistle blowers in the federal civil service: new evidence of the public service ethic', *Journal of Public Administration Research and Theory*, 8(3), 413–440.

Brighouse, H. (2000) *School Choice and Social Justice* (New York: Oxford University Press).

Brown, G. (2003) 'A Modern Agenda for Prosperity and Social Reform', available at http://www.hmtreasury.gov.uk/newsroom_and_speeches/press/2003/press_12_03.cfm, accessed on 3 August 2005.

Buchanan, J. and Tullock, G. (1962) *The Calculus of Consent* (Ann Arbor, MI: University of Michigan Press).

Burgess, S., Propper, C. and Wilson, D. (2005) *Choice: Will More Choice Improve Outcomes in Education and Health Care? Evidence from Economic Research* (Bristol: Centre for Market and Public Organisation).

Callinicos, A. (2000) *Equality* (Cambridge: Polity).

Callinicos. A. (2003) *Against the Third Way* (Cambridge: Polity).

Carvel, J. (2004) 'Low turnout in hospital vote', *The Guardian*, April 7.

Chaloupka, F.J. and Corbett, M. (1998) 'Trade Policy and Tobacco: Towards an Optimal Policy Mix', in Abedian, I., van der Merwe, R., Wilkins, N. and Jha, P. (eds) *The Economics of Tobacco Control: Towards an Optimal Policy Mix* (Cape Town, South Africa: Applied Fiscal Research Centre), 129–145.

Chan, D. and Gan Goh, L. (2000) 'The doctor-patient relationship: a survey of attitudes and practices of doctors in Singapore', *Bioethics*, 14(1), 58–76.

Chen, S. (2003) *Fifth Pillar – Active Citizenship and Public Service Reform* (London: Social Market Foundation).

Chin, J.J. (2002) 'Doctor-patient relationship: from medical paternalism to enhanced autonomy', *Singapore Medical Journal*, 43(3), 152–155.

Clarke, J. and Vidler, E. (2004) 'The contradictions of consumerism: remaking public services', paper presented at the Political Studies Association Conference, 6 April.

Clinton, B. (2003) *A Plan for the Future*, available at http://www.third-way.info/BlairClinton.html, accessed on 3 August2005.

Coates, D. (2000) *Models of Capitalism: Growth and Stagnation in the Modern Era* (Cambridge: Polity).

Collin, J. and Lee, K. (2003) *Globalisation and Transborder Health Risk in the UK. Case Studies in Tobacco Control and Population Mobility* (London: The Nuffield Trust).

138 *References*

Cohen, J. and Rogers, J. (1995) *Associations and Democracy* (New York: Verso).

Commission on Public Private Partnerships (2001) *Building Better Partnerships: The Final Report of the Commission on Public Private Partnerships* (London: Institute for Public Policy Research).

Commission on Taxation and Citizenship (2000) *Paying for Progress: A New Politics Of Tax For Public Spending* (London: The Fabian Society).

Coote, A. and Hunter, D.J. (1996) *New Agenda for Health* (London: Institute for Public Policy Research).

Corrigan, P. and Steele, J. (2001a) *The Case for the Public Interest Company: A New Form of Enterprise for Public Service Delivery* (London: Public Management Foundation).

Corrigan, P. and Steele, J. (2001b) *What Makes a Public Service Public?* (London: Public Management Foundation).

Corry, D. and Stoker (2002) *New Localism. Refashioning the Centre-local Relationship* (London: New Local Government Network).

Corry, D., Emmerich, M. and Stoker, G. (2003) 'The Conundrums of Public Service Reform: Prescription or Evolution, Choice or Uniformity, Central Control or Local Direction', *Renewal,* 11(3), 50–60.

Coulter, A. (2002) *The Autonomous Patient: Ending Paternalism in Medical Care* (London: The Nuffield Trust).

Coulter, A. and Magee, H. (eds) (2004) *The European Patient of the Future,* (Maidenhead: Open University Press).

Cowan, R., David, P.A. and Foray, D. (2000) 'The explicit economics of knowledge and tacitness', *Industrial and Corporate Change*, 9(2), 211–253.

Crescenti, M. (1999) 'The new tobacco world', *Tobacco Journal International*, March, 51–53.

Crewson, P.E. (1997) 'Public service motivation: building empirical evidence of incidence and effect', *Journal of Public Administration Research and Theory* 7(4), 499—518.

Crosland, C.A.R. (1985) [1956] *The Future of Socialism* (London: Jonathan Cape).

Crouch, C. (2003) *Commercialisation or Citizenship: Education Policy And The Future of Public Services* (London: Fabian Society).

Crouch, C. and Streeck, W. (1997) 'Preface', in Crouch, C. and Streeck, W. (ed.) *Political Economy of Modern Capitalism. Mapping Convergence and Diversity* (London: Sage), ix–x.

Disney, H. (2004) (ed.) *Impatient for Change: European Attitudes to Healthcare Reform* (London: Stockholm Network and Profile Books).

Dixon, A., Le Grand, J., Henderson, J., Murray, R. and Poteliakhoff, E. (2003) *Is the NHS Equitable? A Review of the Evidence*, Health and Social Care Discussion Paper no. 11 (London: London School of Economics).

Dobson, A. (2004) *Citizenship and the Environment* (Oxford: Oxford University Press).

Donelan, K., Blendon, R.J., Schoen, C., Davis, K. and Binns, K. (1999) 'The cost of health system change: public discontent in five nations', *Health Affairs*, 18(3), 206–216.

Donelan, K., Blendon, R.J., Schoen, C., Binns, K., Osborn, R. and Davis, K. (2000) 'The elderly in five nations: the importance of universal coverage', *Health Affairs*, 19(3), 226–235.

Drèze, J. and Sen, A. (1997) *India: Economic Development and Social Opportunity*, (Delhi: Oxford University Press).

Dworkin, R. (2000) *Sovereign Value. The Theory and Practice of Equality* (Cambridge, MA: Harvard University Press).

Economist (1998) 'Goldilocks politics', 19 December Employee Benefit Research Institute (2002) *Choice in Health Care*, fact sheet from Health Confidence Survey (Washington, DC: Employee Benefit Research Institute).

Evandrou, M., Falkingham. J., Le Grand, J. and Winter, D. (1992) 'Equity in health and social care', *Journal of Social Policy*, 21(4), 489–523.

Faller, H. (2003) 'Shared decision-making: an approach to strengthening patient participation in rehabilitation', *Rehabilitation*, 42(3), 129–135.

Faulks, K. (1998) *Citizenship in Modern Britain* (Edinburgh: Edinburgh University Press).

Faux, J. (1999) 'Lost on the third way', *Dissent*, 46(2), 67–76.

Fiske, T. and Ladd, H. (2000) *When Schools Compete: A Cautionary Tale* (Washington, DC: The Brookings Institution).

Fiske, T. and Ladd, H. (2001) 'The uneven playing field of school choice: evidence from New Zealand', *Journal of Policy Analysis and Management*, 20(1), 43–64.

Forster, D. (1976) 'Social class differences in sickness and in general practitioner consultations', *Health Trends*, 8, 29–32.

Frey, B. and Oberholzer-Gee, F. (1997) 'The cost of price incentives: an empirical analysis of motivation crowding out', *American Economic Review*, 87, 746–755.

Fukuda-Parr, S. (2002) 'Operationalising Amartya Sen's ideas on capabilities, development, freedom and human rights – the shifting policy focus of the Human Development Approach', available at http://hdr.undp.org/docs/training/ oxford/readings/fukuda-parr_HDA.pdf, accessed on 14 October 2005.

Fuller, B., Elmore, R. and Oldfield, G. (eds) (1996) *Who Chooses? Who Loses?* (New York: Teachers College Press).

Fung, A. and Wright, E.O. (2001) 'Deepening democracy: innovations in empowered participatory governance', *Politics and Society*, 29(1), 5–41.

Fung, A. and Wright, E.O. (eds) (2003) *Deepening Democracy: Innovations in Empowered Participatory Governance* (New York: Verso).

Gamble, A. (1996) *Hayek: The Iron Cage of Liberty* (Cambridge: Polity).

Gamble, A. (2000) *Politics and Fate* (Cambridge: Polity).

Gamble, A. and Kelly, G. (1996) 'The Politics of Ownership', *New Left Review*, no. 220, Nov/Dec, 62–97.

Gamble, A. and Kelly, G. (2000) 'The Politics of the Company', in Parkinson, J. Gamble, A. and Kelly, G. (eds) *The Political Economy of the Company* (Oxford: Hart), 21–49.

Gamble, A. and Paxton, W. (2005) 'Democracy, Social Justice and the State', in Pearce, N. and Paxton, W. (eds) *Social Justice: Building a Fairer Britain* (London: Politicos), 11 219–239.

Gamble, A. and Wright. T. (2004) 'Introduction', in Gamble. A. and Wright, T. (eds) *Restating the State?* (Oxford: Blackwell in association with the Political Quarterly), 1–10.

Gatrell, A., Garnett, S., Rigby, J., Maddocks, A. and Kirwan, M. (1998) 'Uptake of screening for breast cancer in south Lancashire', *Public Health*, 112(5), 297–301.

Giddens, A. (1998) *The Third Way: The Renewal of Social Democracy* (Cambridge: Polity).

Giddens, A. (2000) *The Third Way and Its Critics* (Cambridge: Polity).

Giddens, A. (2001) *The Global Third Way Debate* (Cambridge: Polity).

Goddard, M. and Smith, P. (2001) 'Equity of access to health care services', *Social Science and Medicine*, 53(9), 1149–1162.

Goldthorpe, J.H. (ed.) (1984) *Order and Conflict in Contemporary Capitalism* (Oxford: Clarendon Press).

Grout, P. and Stevens, M. (2003) 'The assessment: financing and managing public services', *Oxford Review of Economic Policy*, 19(2), 215–234.

Guy Peters, B. (2004) 'Back to the Centre? Rebuilding the State', in Gamble, A. and Wright, T. (eds) *Rebuilding the State* (Oxford: Blackwell), 130–140.

Hall, P.A. (1986) *Governing the Economy: The Politics of State Intervention in Britain and France* (New York: Oxford University Press).

Hall, S. (1998) 'The great moving nowhere show', *Marxism Today*, November/December, 9–14.

Ham, C. and Alberti, K.G.M.M. (2002), 'The medical profession, the public and the government', *British Medical Journal*, 324, 6 April, 838–842.

Handler, J. (2004) *Social Citizenship and Workfare in the United States and Western Europe. The Paradox of Inclusion* (Cambridge: Cambridge University Press).

Harris, M. (1998) 'The New Right', in Lent, A. (ed.) *New Political Thought: An Introduction* (London: Lawrence and Wishart), 53–71.

Hart, O. (1995) 'Corporate governance: some theory and implications', *Economic Journal*, 105, 678–689.

Hay, C. (1999) *The Political Economy of New Labour: Labouring under False Pretences?* (Manchester: Manchester University Press).

Hayek, F.A. (1949) *Individualism and Economic Order* (London: Routledge and Kegan Paul).

Hayek, F.A. (1960) *The Constitution of Liberty* (Chicago: The University of Chicago Press).

Hayek, F.A. (1967) *Studies in Philosophy, Politics and Economics* (London: Routledge and Kegan Paul).

Hayek, F.A. (1976) [1952] *The Sensory Order: An Inquiry into the Foundations of Theoretical Psychology* (London: Routledge and Kegan Paul).

Hayek, F.A. (1978) 'Competition as a Discovery Procedure', in Hayek, F. (ed.) *New Studies in Philosophy, Politics, Economics and the History of Ideas* (London: Routledge and Kegan Paul), 179–190.

Hayek, F.A. (1998)[1976] *Law, Legislation and Liberty: A New Statement of the Liberal Principles of Justice and Political Economy: Volume 2 The Mirage of Social Justice* (London: Routledge).

Hayek, F.A. (2002) [1944] *The Road to Serfdom* (London: Routledge).

Hayes, M. (1994) *The New Right in Britain: An Introduction To Theory And Practice*, (London: Pluto Press).

Held, D. Goldblatt, D. McGrew, A. and Perraton, J. (1999) *Global Transformations: Politics, Economics and Culture* (Cambridge: Polity).

Hemingway, H., Saunders, D. and Parsons, L. (1997) 'Social class, spoken language and pattern of care as determinants of continuity of carer in maternity services in east London', *Journal of Public Health Medicine*, 19(2), 156–161.

Hill, P.T. (2002) 'Introduction', in P.T. Hill (ed.) *Choice with Equity* (Stanford: The Hoover Institution), 1–14.

Hill, P.T. and Guin, K. (2002) 'Baselines for Assessment of Choice Programs', in Hill, P.T. Hill (ed.) *Choice with Equity* (Stanford: The Hoover Institution), 15–49.

Hirst, P. (1996)[1994] *Associative Democracy: New Forms of Economic and Social Governance* (Cambridge: Polity).

Hirst, P. and Thompson, G. (1996) *Globalization in Question: The International Economy and the Possibility of Governance* (Cambridge: Polity).

Hirst, P. (1999a) 'Associationalist welfare: a reply to Marc Stears', *Economy and Society*, 28(4), 590–597.

Hirst, P. (1999b) 'Globalisation and social democracy', in Gamble, A. and Wright, T. (ed.) *The New Social Democracy* (Oxford: Blackwell), 84–96.

Hodgson, G. (1999) *Economic and Utopia: Why the Learning Economy Is Not the End of History* (London: Routledge).

Holtham, G. and Kay, J. (1994) 'The assessment: institutions of policy', *Oxford Review of Economic Policy*, 10(3), 1–16.

Hoxby, C. (2003a) 'School choice and school competition: evidence from the United States', *Swedish Economic Policy*, 10, 11–67.

Hoxby, C. (2003b) 'School choice and school productivity (or, is school choice a rising tide that lifts all boats?)', in Hoxby, C. (ed.) *The Economic Analysis of School Choice* (Chicago: University of Chicago Press), 287–341.

Ioannides, S. (2000) 'Austrian economics, socialism and impure forms of economic organisation', *Review of Political Economy* 12(1), 45–71.

Ironside, M. and Seifert, R. (2004) 'Public sector workers: delivering the services and servicing the deliverers', paper delivered at 2004 Political Studies Association Conference at the University of Lincoln. Irvine, C. and Gratzer, D. (2002) *Medicare and User Fees: Unsafe at Any Price?*, Atlantic Institute for Market Studies (AIMS) Health Care Reform Background Paper number 9 (Halifax, Nova Scotia: AIMS).

Jayasuriya, K. (2000) 'Capability, Freedom and the New Social Democracy', *Political Quarterly*, 71(3), 282–299.

Jenkinson, T. (2003) 'Private Finance', *Oxford Review of Economic Policy* 19(2), 323–334.

Johnson, B., Lorenz, E. and Lundvall, B.A. (2002) 'Why all this fuss about codified and tacit knowledge?', *Industrial and Corporate Change* 11(2), 245–262.

Joossens, L. and Rattiphakde, B. (2000) 'Role of multinationals and other private actors: trade and investment practices', paper presented to World Health Organization International Conference on Global Tobacco Control Law, New Delhi, 7–9 January.

Jowitt, J. (2004) 'Congestion charging sweeps the world', *The Observer*, February 15.

Kay, J. (1996) 'The Future of UK Utility Regulation', in Beesley. M.E. (ed.) *Regulating Utilities: A Time for Change?* (London: Institute of Economic Affairs), 145—175.

Kay, J. (1997) 'The Stakeholder Corporation', in Kelly, G., Kelly, D and Gamble, A. (eds) *Stakeholder Capitalism* (Basingstoke: Macmillan), 125–141.

Kelly, G. and Parkinson, J. (2001) 'The Conceptual Foundations of the Company: a Pluralist Approach', in Parkinson, J., Gamble, A. and Kelly, G. (eds) *The Political Economy of the Company* (London: Hart Publishing), 113–139.

142

References

Khunti, K., Ganguli, S. and Lowy, A. (2001) 'Inequalities in provision of systematic care for patients with diabetes', *Family Practictioner*, 18(1), 27–32.

Kildal, N. (2001) *Workfare Tendencies in Scandinavian Welfare Policies* (Geneva: International Labour Office).

King, D. and Wickham-Jones, D. (1999) 'From Clinton to Blair: The Democratic (Party) Origins of Welfare to Work', *Political Quarterly*, 70, 62–74.

King, D. and Wood, S. (1999) 'The Political Economy of Neoliberalism: Britain and the United States in the 1980s', in Kitschelt, H., Lange, P., Marks, G. and Stephens, J.D. (eds) *Continuity and Change in Contemporary Capitalism* (Cambridge: Cambridge University Press), 371–397.

Kirzner, I. (1988) 'The economic calculation debates: lessons for Austrians', *Review of Austrian Economics*, 2(1), 1–18.

Kitschelt, H., Lange, P., Marks, G. and Stephens, J.D. (eds)(1999) *Continuity and Change in Contemporary Capitalism* (Cambridge: Cambridge University Press).

Knight, E., Ayers, P. and Mayer, G. (1998) *The U.S. Tobacco Industry in Domestic and World Markets* (Washington, DC: Congressional Research Service).

Koppell, J. (2003) *The Politics of Quasi-government* (Cambridge: Cambridge University Press).

Kotlikoff, L.J. and Burns, S. (2004) *The Coming Generational Storm: What You Need to Know about America's Economic Future* (Cambridge, MA: MIT Press).

Krugman, P. (2005) 'America's senior moment', *New York Review of Books*, March 10, 6–11.

Ladd, H. (2002) 'School vouchers: a critical view', *Journal of Economic Perspectives*, 16(4), 3–24.

Lambrew, J. (2005) *'Choice' in Health Care: What Do People Really Want?*, Issue Brief (New York: Commonwealth Fund).

Lange, O. (1938) 'On the Economic Theory of Socialism', reprinted in Lippicott, B. (ed.) (1964) *On the Economic Theory of Socialism* (Minneapolis: University of Minnesota Press), 57–143.

Lavoie, D. (1985) *Rivalry and Central Planning: The Socialist Calculation Debates Reconsidered* (Cambridge: Cambridge University Press).

Leadbeater, C. (2000) *Living on Thin Air: The New Economy* (London: Penguin).

Lee, K. (2003) *Globalization and Health: An Introduction* (Basingstoke: Palgrave).

Le Grand, J. (1978) 'The distribution of public expenditure: the case of health care', *Economica*, 45, 124–142.

Le Grand, J. (2003a) 'The least worst way to improve public services: the case of competition', *Renewal* 11(2), 29–33.

Le Grand, J. (2003b) *Motivation, Agency and Public Policy: Of Knights & Knaves, Pawns & Queens* (Oxford: Oxford University Press).

Lent, A. and Arend, N. (2004) *Making Choices: How Can Choice Improve Local Public Services?* (London: New Local Government Network).

Levitas, R. (1998) *The Inclusive Society? Social Exclusion and New Labour* (Basingstoke: Macmillan).

Leys, C. (2001) *Market-Driven Politics. Neoliberal Democracy and the Public Interest* (New York: Verso).

Lister, R. (1997) *Citizenship: Feminist Perspectives* (Basingstoke: Palgrave).

Machin, S. and McNally, S. (2003) 'The Literacy Hour', Centre for the Economics of Education, mimeo.

Magnus, J. and Morgan, M. (1999) 'Lessons from the Tacit Knowledge Experiment', in Magnus, J. and Morgan, M. (eds) *Methodology and Tacit Knowledge: Two Experiments In Econometrics* (London: John Wiley), 375–381.

Maltby (2003a) *In the Public Interest? Assessing the Potential of Public Interest Companies* (London: Institute for Public Policy Research).

Maltby, P. (2003b) *Public Interest Companies and Four Principles of Public Service Reform: A Paper for the Office of Public Service Reform* (London: Institute for Public Policy Research).

Maltby, P. and Gosling, T. (2003) *Ending the 'Two-tier Workforce'* (London: Institute for Public Policy Research).

Marquand, D. (1988) *The Unprincipled Society: New Demands and Old Politics*, (London: Jonathan Cape).

Marquand, D. (1996) 'Moralists and Hedonists', in Marquand, D. and Seldon, A. (eds) *The Ideas that Shaped Post-War Britain* (London: Fontana Press), 5–28.

Marquand, D. (1997) *The New Reckoning: Capitalism, States and Citizens* (Cambridge: Polity).

Marquand, D. (2004) *Decline of the Public* (Cambridge: Polity).

Marshall, T.H. (1992) [1950] 'Citizenship and Social Class', in Marshall, T.H. and Bottomore, T. (ed.) *Citizenship and Social Class* (London: Pluto Press), 3–51.

Mayo, E. and Moore, H. (2001) *The Mutual State: How Local Communities Can Run Public Services* (London: New Economics Foundation).

Mead, L (1986) *Beyond Entitlement: The Social Obligations Of Citizenship* (New York: Free Press).

Miers, T. (2003) 'The Magic of Choice: Reaping The Full Benefits Of Competition In Public Services', available at http:\\www.iea.org.uk/files/upld-news85pdf?.pdf, accessed on 10 April 2006.

Millar, F. (2004) 'The other "c" word', *The Guardian*, 17 February.

Miller, D. (2000) *Citizenship and National Identity*, (Cambridge: Polity).

Miller, D. (2005) 'What is Social Justice?', in Pearce, N. and Paxton, W. (eds) *Social Justice: Building a Fairer Britain* (London: Politicos), 3–20.

Mises, L. (1920) 'Economic Calculation in the Socialist Commonwealth', reprinted in Hayek, F. (ed.)(1935) *Collectivist Economic Planning* (London: Routledge), 87–130.

Moe, T. (2002) 'The Structure of School Choice', in Hill, P.T. (ed.) *Choice with Equity* (Stanford: The Hoover Institution).

Needham, C. (2003) *Citizen-Consumers: New Labour's Marketplace Democracy*, (London: Catalyst).

Nonaka, I. and Takeuchi, H. (1995) *The Knowledge Creating Company: How Japanese Companies Create the Dynamics of Innovation* (Oxford: Oxford University Press).

Nozick, R. (1974) *Anarchy, State and Utopia* (New York: Basic Books).

Nussbaum, M. (2000) *Women and Human Development: The Capabilities Approach* (Cambridge: Cambridge University Press).

Nussbaum, M. (2001) *Upheavals of Thought. The Intelligence of Emotions* (Cambridge: Cambridge University Press).

O'Donnell, O., Propper, C. and Upward, R. (1991) *An Empirical Study of Equity in the Finance and Delivery of Health Care in Britain* (York: University of York).

Ohmae, K. (1990) *The Borderless World: Power and Strategy in the Interlinked Economy* (London: Fontana).

Organization for Economic Co-operation and Development (1996) *Ageing in OECD Countries* (Paris: Organization for Economic Co-operation and Development).

Organization for Economic Co-operation and Development (2004a) *OECD in Figures. 2004 Edition. Statistics on the Member Countries* (Paris: OECD).

Organization for Economic Co-operation and Development (2004b) *Towards High-Performing Health Systems* (Paris: Organization for Economic Co-operation and Development)

Parkinson, J.E. (1993) *Corporate Power and Responsibility. Issues in the Theory of Company Law* (Oxford: Oxford University Press).

Pendleton, A. (1997) 'Stakeholders as Shareholders: The Role of Employee Share Ownership', in Kelly, G., Kelly, D. and Gamble, A. (eds) (1997) *'Stakeholder Capitalism'* (Basingstoke: Macmillan), 169–182.

Pennington, M. (2003) 'Hayekian Political Economy and the Limits of Deliberative Democracy', *Political Studies*, 51, 722–739.

Penrose, E. (1959) *The Theory of the Growth of the Firm*, Oxford, Basil Blackwell.

Perri 6 (2003) 'Giving consumers of British public services more choice: what can be learned from recent history?', *Journal of Social Policy,* 32(2), 239–270.

Pettit, P. (1999) *Republicanism: A Theory Of Freedom And Government* (Oxford: Clarendon Press).

Pierson, C. (2001) *Hard Choices: Social Democracy in the 21st Century* (Cambridge: Polity).

Plant. R. (1996) 'Social Democracy', in Marquand, D. and Seldon, A. (eds) *The Ideas That Shaped Post-war Britain* (London: Fontana Press), 139–164.

Plant, R. (2003) 'A public service ethic and political accountability', *Parliamentary Affairs*, 56(4), 560–579.

Prentice, S. (2002) 'People, not structures, hold the key to public service reform', *Renewal,* 10(3), 48–57.

Propper, C. and Wilson, D. (2003) 'The use and usefulness of performance measures in the public sector', *Oxford Review of Economic Policy*, 19(2), 250–267.

Quill, T.E. and Brody, H. (1996) 'Finding a balance between physician power and patient choice', *Annals of Internal Medicine*, 125(9), 763–769.

Redwood, J. (2002) *Third Way – Which Way? How Should We Pay for Public Services* (London: Middlesex University Press).

Reich, R. (1999) 'We are all Third Wayers now', *American Prospect*, available at http://www.prospect.org/print/V10/43/reich-r.html, accessed on 11 April 2006.

Richards, H.M., Reid, M. E. and Watt, G.C.M. (2002) 'Socioeconomic variations in responses to chest pain: qualitative study', *British Medical Journal*, 324(1), June, 1308–1310.

Robinson, P. (2004) *How Do We Pay? The Funding of Public Services in the EU* (Institute for Public Policy Research and The Centre: London and Brussels).

Ryle, G. (2000) [1949] *The Concept of Mind* (London: Penguin).

Sako, M. (1999) 'From individual skills to organizational capability in Japan', *Oxford Review of Economic Policy*, 15(1), 114–126.

Scholte, J.A. (2000) *Globalization: A Critical Introduction* (Basingstoke: Macmillan).

Schwartz, B. (2003) *Paradox of Choice: Why More Is Less* (New York: Harpercollins).

Seidman, H. (1952) 'The theory of the autonomous government corporation: a critical appraisal', *Public Administration Review*, 12(2), 89–96.

Seidman, H. (1954) 'The government corporation: organization and controls', *Public Administration Review*, 14(3), 183–192.

Selznick, P. (1953) *TVA and the Grass Roots: A Study in the Sociology of Formal Organization* (Berkeley: University of California Press).

Sen, A. (1984) *Resources, Values and Development* (Cambridge, MA: MIT Press).

Sen, A. (1985) *Commodities and Capabilities* (Amsterdam: North Holland).

Sen, A. (1987) *On Ethics and Economics* (Oxford: Blackwell).

Sen, A. (1999) *Development as Freedom* (Oxford: Oxford University Press).

Seymour, D.G. and Garthwaite, P.H. (1999) 'Age, deprivation and rates of inguinal hernia surgery in men. Is there inequity of access to healthcare?', *Age Aging*, 28(5), 485–490.

Sherraden, M. (2003) 'Assets and the Social Investment State', in Paxton, W. (ed.) *Equal Shares? Building a Progressive and Coherent Asset-Based Welfare Policy*, (London: Institute for Public Policy Research), 28–41.

Shonfield, A. (1965) *Modern Capitalism: The Changing Balance of Public and Private Power* (New York: Oxford University Press).

Skidelsky, R. (1996) 'The fall of Keynesian: a historian's view', in Marquand, D. and Seldon, A. (eds) *The Ideas That Shaped Post-war Britain* (London: Fontana Press) 41–66.

Sternberg, E. (1998) *Corporate Governance: Accountability in the Marketplace* (London: Institute of Economic Affairs).

Stoker, G. (2003) 'New Labour needs local government', *Renewal*, 11(1), 61–67.

Stoker, G. (2004) 'New localism, progressive politics and democracy', in Gamble, A. and Wright, T. (eds) *Restating the State?* (Oxford: Blackwell in association with the Political Quarterly), 117–129.

Sutton, M., Gravelle, H., Morris, S., Leyland, A., Windmeijer, F. and Dibben, C. (2002) 'Allocation of Resources to English Areas: Individual and Small Area Determinants of Morbidity and Use of Health Care Resources Report', Report to the Department of Health (Edinburgh: Information and Services Division).

Tawney, R.H. (1931) *Equality* (London: Allen & Unwin).

Tawney, R.H. (1948)[1920] *The Acquisitive Society* (London: Harcourt Bruce and Jovanovich).

Titmuss, R. (1971) *The Gift Relationship* (London: Allen and Unwin).

Tivey, L. (1978) *The Politics of the Firm* (Oxford: Martin Robertson).

Tomlinson, J. (1990) *Hayek and the Market* (London: Pluto Press).

Unison (2004) *Fair Wages: How to End the Two-tier Workforce in Public Services* available at http://www.unison.org.uk/acrobat/B1433.pdf, accessed on 12 April 2006.

United Nations (2005) *Human Development Report. International Cooperation at a Crossroads: Aid, Trade and Security in an Unequal World* (New York: Human Development Report Office).

Van Doorslaer, E. and Masseria, C. (2004) *Income-related Inequality in the Use of Medical Care in 21 OECD Countries*, Health Working Paper number 14 (Paris: OECD).

Van Doorslaer, E., Koolman, X. and Puffer, F. (2002) 'Equity in the use of physician visits in OECD countries: has equal treatment for equal need been achieved?', in Organization for Economic Co-operation and Development (ed.) *Measuring Up: Improving Health Systems Performance in OECD Countries* (Paris: OECD), 225–248.

Verba, S., Schlozman, K.L. and Brady, H.E. (1995) *Voice and Equality: Civic Voluntarism in American Politics* (Cambridge, MA: Harvard University Press).

Wainwright, H. (2003) *Reclaim the State: Experiments in Popular Democracy* (New York: Verso).

Walker, D. (2002) *In Praise of Centralism: A Critique of The New Localism*, (London: Catalyst).

Walzer, M. (1983) *Spheres of Justice: A Defence of Pluralism and Equality* (New York: Basic Books).

Wells, A.S. (1993) *Time to Choose: America at the Crossroads of School Choice Policy* (New York: Hill and Wang).

White, S. (1997) 'What Do Egalitarians Want?', in Franklin, J. (eds) *Equality* (London: Institute for Public Policy Research) 59–82.

White, S. (1998) 'Interpreting the third way: not one route but many', *Renewal*, 6(2), 17–30.

White, S. (2000) 'Social rights and the social contract – political theory and the new welfare politics', *British Journal of Political Science*, 30, 507–532.

White, S. (2003) *The Civic Minimum: On the Rights and Obligations of Economic Citizenship* (Oxford: Oxford University Press).

Willetts, D. (1997) 'The poverty of stakeholding', in Kelly, G., Kelly, D. and Gamble, A. (eds), *Stakeholder Capitalism* (London: Macmillan), 20–28.

Working Commission on Choice in K-12 Education (2004) *School Choice. Doing it the Right Way Makes a Difference* (Washington, DC: The Brookings Institution).

World Bank (1994) *Averting the Old Age Crisis* (New York: Oxford University Press).

Wright, E.O. (1998) 'Introduction', Wright, E.O. (ed.) *Recasting Egalitarianism: New Rules for Communities, States and Markets* (New York: Verso), xi–xiii.

Index